Industrial IoT Application Architectures and Use Cases

Industrial IoT Application Architectures and Use Cases

A. Suresh

Malarvizhi Nandagopal

Pethuru Raj

E. A. Neeba

Jenn-Wei Lin

CRC Press
Taylor & Francis Group
Boca Raton London New York

CRC Press is an imprint of the
Taylor & Francis Group, an **informa** business

AN AUERBACH BOOK

CRC Press
Taylor & Francis Group
6000 Broken Sound Parkway NW, Suite 300
Boca Raton, FL 33487-2742

© 2020 by Taylor & Francis Group, LLC
CRC Press is an imprint of Taylor & Francis Group, an Informa business

Printed on acid-free paper
International Standard Book Number-13: 978-0-367-34308-8 (Hardback)

Visit the Taylor & Francis Web site at
http://www.taylorandfrancis.com

and the CRC Press Web site at
http://www.crcpress.com

Contents

Preface

Through a bevy of proven and potential digitization and edge technologies, all our physical, mechanical, and electrical systems are getting digitized. Digitized objects are able to find, bind, and leverage the unique capacities and capabilities of one another in their vicinity and with remote ones through one or more networks. That is, they are destined to join in the mainstream computing. The much-discussed context-awareness feature and functionality can be realized and provided through such digitized artifacts and their collaborations. This is the crux of the fast-emerging and evolving concept of the Internet of Things (IoT). That is, all kinds of tangible objects in our everyday environments (homes, hospitals, hotels, etc.) are being technologically enabled to be digitized. It is estimated by market analysts and watchers that there will be trillions of digitized entities in the years to come. Furthermore, all kinds of electronics appliances, equipment, instruments, and machineries are meticulously connected with one another. As a result, we are heading toward billions of connected devices. In addition, devices at ground level are being integrated with cyber/virtualized/containerized applications, services, and databases. That is, various physical systems in our midst are getting formally linked up with remotely-held cloud systems to bring forth futuristic use cases for empowering human beings in their assignments and obligations. This distinguished combination is being portrayed as cyber-physical systems. The deeper and extreme connectivity and integration aspects clearly foretell that all are tending toward a cloud-connected era.

As digitized and connected elements grow exponentially in number, their purposeful interactions are bound to generate a massive amount of multi-structured data. The challenge here is to transition raw data to information and knowledge, which can be used by people and systems to be intelligent in their decisions, deals, and deeds. With the faster maturity and stability of artificial intelligence (AI) algorithms and approaches, knowledge discovery and dissemination out of data heaps get simplified and streamlined. Thus, batch and stream processing of big and real-time data toward the realization of actionable insights in time are being touted as the key challenge for the ensuing era of knowledge. With IoT and CPS data getting carefully collected and crunched to extricate useful and usable information through the smart application of AI technologies and tools, there will be a dazzling array of smarter and sophisticated services and applications. That is, the cognitive era is all set to dawn and beckon us. Precisely speaking, cloudified, connected, and cognitive systems have laid down a stimulating foundation to visualize a fresh set of game-changing and trend-setting applications for the total human society. In this book, we have focused on presenting next-generation use cases of IoT and IoT data analytics for a variety of business verticals.

Chapter 1, The Internet of Things (IoT) Paradigm: The Use Cases, discusses the various personal, social, and industrial use cases of the IoT paradigm. The subsequent chapters will dig deeper and dwell at length on various popular use cases and their real-time applications in everyday human life, where it reduces the manpower and the risk to human beings and safeguards them.

Chapter 2, An Intelligent IoT Framework for Smart Water Management in Agriculture, presents intelligent water management for smart agriculture. In order to accommodate a growing population, the call for more food will increase and new strategies should be designed to create more reliable agricultural production and improve the growing instances of water scarcity.

Chapter 3, IoT-Enabled Smart Traffic Control System for Congestion Control, introduces a smart traffic management system and adjustments that influence a transportation system; for example, the impact on the whole transportation system is influenced by significant enhancements of one corridor. Smart traffic lights have been set up to oversee a stream of traffic, but these are ending up progressively wasteful because of their structure.

Chapter 4, An Intelligent Airport System Using Artificial Intelligence (AI) Algorithm, presents the challenges, characteristics, and best methods for enhancing implementation in smart airports. Airports are regarded as a gateway to any nation. Based on the report of the US Homeland Security Presidential Directive 7 (HSPD-7), airports are considered as a sub-sector of the Transportation Systems Sector and therefore represent an important infrastructure that must be enhanced in terms of surveillance.

Chapter 5, An Effective IoT Framework for the Healthcare Environment, discusses reporting the progress of patients by the available technology used in the healthcare system and how it integrates patient information for their caretakers. This could increase the physical and mental health of patients at minimal cost in less time.

Chapter 6, Fuzzy Scheduling with IoT for Tracking and Monitoring Hotel Assets, utilizes fuzzy scheduling-based intelligent real-time tracking and monitoring of the workers in the smart hotel with the enhanced IoT technology. Here, the IoT is combined with fuzzy scheduling to benefit as maximum for the customers.

Chapter 7, An Effective IoT Drainage System for Detection of Drainage Pipes, presents several techniques in designing an effective drainage system and employing generation and penetration of radar technique for detection of drainage pipes. In recent years, drainage management as well as urban storm drainage in urban infrastructure has gained major importance.

Chapter 8, Predictive Maintenance in IoT for Retail Machine Industries, presents a predictive maintenance approach, which involves direct monitoring of the mechanical condition of plant equipment to decide the actual mean time to malfunction for each preferred machine. The mechanical construction of the equipment will be monitored to estimate the fault that occurred in the machines and to identify the time of the fault.

Chapter 9, Integrating ANN and IoT for Predictive Maintenance in Industries, proposes a method with an Artificial Neural Network (ANN) and IoT that could be best used for prediction purposes when compared to other algorithms since it does the best purpose of function approximation, clustering, and forecasting. Finally, the comparison has been made between ANN and other algorithms in terms of accuracy, precision, and specification.

Chapter 10, IoT Integration in Blockchain for Smart Waste Management, presents techniques based on IoT and blockchain-driven waste management, and deals with effective waste management with the implementation of IoT with the machine learning algorithm that could be highly revolutionary in the management of waste.

Acknowledgments

I express my sincere and heartfelt gratitude to the management concerns of Nehru Group of Institutions, Adv. Dr. P. Krishna Das, Chairman & Managing Trustee, and Dr. P. Krishna Kumar, CEO & Secretary, Nehru Group of Institutions, Coimbatore, for their simplicity, readiness, and supporting tendency inspired in bringing up confidence in taking ideal steps. My sincere thanks to Dr. P. Maniiarasan, Principal, Nehru Institute of Engineering and Technology, T. M. Palayam, Coimbatore, for giving me the privilege and honor to present the technical works beyond my administration and providing invaluable guidance throughout this work.

I would also like to thank R. Udendhran, Department of Computer Science, Bharathidasan University, Trichy, India, a great friend of mine with empathy, dynamism, support, and motivation, who deeply inspired me. I extend my heartfelt thanks to the faculty of Department of Computer Science and Engineering, Nehru Institute of Engineering and Technology, T. M. Palayam, Coimbatore, for their acceptance and patience in sharing work during my preparation, and to my family for their kindness, support, and care.

A. Suresh

First and foremost, I want to offer this endeavor to God Almighty for the wisdom, strength, peace of mind, and good health He bestowed upon me and helped me in finishing this book. I would like to express my deepest gratitude to John Wyzalek, Senior Acquisitions Editor, CRC Press/Taylor & Francis Group, who motivated me to prepare the book contents and accepted to publish this book. I express my hearty thankfulness to him.

I would like to express my sincere and heartfelt gratitude to the institution concerns of Vel Tech Rangarajan Dr. Sagunthala R&D Institute of Science and Technology for providing an immense support in all my endeavors. I take this opportunity to extend my gratitude toward my family for their valuable guidance and continuous support at different stages from the very beginning to completion of this book. Finally, I sincerely convey my appreciation to everyone on the editing, proofreading, and publishing team of CRC Press.

Malarvizhi Nandagopal

I solemnly submit here my profound gratitude to my managers, Anish Shah and Kiran Thomas, the President at Reliance Industries Limited, Bombay, for their moral support. I also appreciate my former manager, Sreekrishnan Venkateswaran, distinguished engineer (DE), IBM Cloud, for all the enchanting technical discussions. I appreciate my colleagues, Senthil Arunachalam and Vidya Hungud, for their cooperation.

At this moment, I reflect the selfless sacrifices of my parents during my formative days. I thank my wife, Sweetlin Reena, and my sons, Darren Samuel and Darresh Bernie, for their extreme patience. Above all, I give all the glory and honor to my Lord and Savior, Jesus Christ, for granting the physical strength and the knowledge required toward contributing something for this book.

Pethuru Raj

At first, I would like to thank Almighty God, the author of knowledge and wisdom, who made this possible. I avail this opportunity to extend sincere thanks to my management, Rajagiri School of Engineering & Technology, Kochi, for the support rendered in completing this book. I remain thankful to all my friends and persons who helped me in different ways directly or indirectly at different stages of my work.

I would fail in my duty if I fall short of words to express my gratitude to my parents, Valsa Abi and I. Abi, for all the unconditional love and amazing chances they have given me over the years. I wish to express my love and affection to my son, Joel John, for his kind patience and encouragement.

E. A. Neeba

I express my sincere gratitude to all coauthors of this book for their big contribution in this book. In addition, I also thank the reviewers and editors for their valuable comments and suggestions to publish this book.

Jenn-Wei Lin

About the Authors

A. Suresh, B.E., M. Tech., Ph.D., is Professor and Head at the Department of Computer Science and Engineering, Nehru Institute of Engineering & Technology, Coimbatore, Tamil Nadu, India. He has nearly two decades of experience in teaching and his areas of specializations are Data Mining, Artificial Intelligence, Image Processing, Multimedia, and System Software. He has two patents and published 85 papers in international journals. He has written five chapters in the book, *An Intelligent Grid Network Based on Cloud Computing Infrastructures,* published by IGI Global Publisher. He has published more than 40 papers in national and international conferences. He has served as an editor/reviewer for Springer, Elsevier, Wiley, Inderscience journals, etc. He is a member of ISTE, MCSI, IACSIT, IAENG, MCSTA, and Global Member of the Internet Society (ISOC). He has organized several National Workshop, Conferences, and Technical Events. He is regularly invited to deliver lectures in various programs for imparting skills in research methodology to students and research scholars. He has authored four books, *Data Structures & Algorithms, Computer Programming, Problem Solving,* and *Python Programming and Programming in "C"* published by DD Publications, Excel Publications, and Sri Maruthi Publisher, Chennai, respectively. He has hosted two special sessions for IEEE-sponsored conferences in Osaka, Japan, and Thailand.

E-mail: prisu6esh@yahoo.com

Malarvizhi Nandagopal, B.E., M.E., Ph.D., is Professor at the Department of Computer Science and Engineering, Vel Tech Rangarajan Dr. Sagunthala R&D Institute of Science and Technology, Chennai, Tamil Nadu, India. She has more than 18 years of teaching experience. She has written a book, *Computer Architecture and Organization,* published by Eswar Press,

The Science and Technology Book Publisher, Chennai. She serves as a reviewer for many reputed journals. She has published numerous papers in International Conferences and Journals. Her area of interest includes Parallel and Distributed Computing, Grid Computing, Cloud Computing, Big Data Analytics, Internet of Things, Computer Architecture, and Operating Systems. She is a life member of Computer Society of India (CSI), Indian Society for Technical Education (ISTE), IARCS, and IAENG. She is a Senior Member of IEEE and IEEE Women in Engineering (WIE). She is a member of Association for Computing Machinery (ACM) and the Institution of Engineering and Technology (IET).

E-mail: drnmalarvizhi@gmail.com

Pethuru Raj, Ph.D., is the Chief Architect at the Site Reliability Engineering (SRE) Center of Excellence, Reliance Infocomm, Ltd. (RIL), Bangalore. He previously worked as a Cloud Infrastructure Architect in the IBM Global Cloud Center of Excellence (CoE), IBM India Bangalore for 4 years. Prior to that, he had a long stint as TOGAF (The Open Group Architecture Framework)-certified Enterprise Architecture (EA) Consultant in Wipro Consulting Services (WCS) Division. He also worked as a Lead Architect in the corporate research (CR) division of Robert Bosch, Bangalore. In total, he has gained more than 17 years of IT industry experience and 8 years of research experience. He obtained his Ph.D. through the CSIR-sponsored Ph.D. degree program in Anna University, Chennai, and continued the UGC-sponsored postdoctoral research in the Department of Computer Science and Automation, Indian Institute of Science, Bangalore. Thereafter, he was granted a couple of international research fellowships (JSPS and JST) to work as a research scientist for 3.5 years in two leading Japanese universities. Regarding publications, he has more than 30 research papers in peer-reviewed journals published by IEEE, ACM, Springer-Verlag, Inderscience, etc. He has authored seven books thus far and focuses on some of the emerging technologies, such as IoT, Cognitive Analytics, Blockchain, Digital Twin, Docker-Enabled Containerization, Data Science, Microservices Architecture, etc. He has contributed 25 book chapters thus far for various technology books edited by highly acclaimed and accomplished professors and professionals. He released his first book, *Cloud Enterprise Architecture*, in 2012, published by CRC Press, USA, and the book details can also be found at the following link: https://crcpress.com/9781466502321. He has edited and authored a book, *Cloud Infrastructures for Big Data Analytics*, published by IGI International, USA, in March 2014. A new book, *Smarter Cities: The Enabling Technologies and Tools*, by CRC Press, USA, hit the market in June 2015. He collaborated with a few authors to write a book titled *High-Performance Big Data Analytics*, published by Springer-Verlag, in 2015.

E-mail: peterindia@gmail.com

E. A. Neeba, M.Tech, Ph.D., is an Assistant Professor at the Department of Information Technology, Rajagiri School of Engineering & Technology, Kochi, Kerala, which is affiliated to the A. P. J. Abdul Kalam Technological University, Kerala. She received her doctoral degree from the Vel Tech Rangarajan Dr. Sagunthala R&D Institute of Science and Technology, Chennai, Tamil Nadu. She completed her masters in Computer Science & Engineering from SRM Institute of Science and Technology, Chennai. Her research interests include Analysis of Data, Data Mining and Big Data, Knowledge Representation, and Ontology, both from the theoretical perspective and their application to natural language understanding, reasoning, information visualization, and interoperability. Having a rich industrial experience of around 10 years prior to joining academia, she also has publications in around 10 SCI/SCIE/Scopus indexed international journals and a few national journals. An active participant in various conferences and workshops on data mining, she is currently involved in several projects in this field. She was entrusted with leadership positions such as the Accreditation Coordinator for the college and Head of the Quality Cell besides organizing various national and international events.

E-mail: neebarset@gmail.com

Jenn-Wei Lin, Ph.D., is a Full Professor at the Department of Computer Science and Information Engineering, Fu Jen Catholic University, Taiwan. He received his M.S. degree in Computer and Information Science from National Chiao Tung University, Hsinchu, Taiwan, in 1993, and his Ph.D. degree in Electrical Engineering from National

Taiwan University, Taipei, Taiwan, in 1999. He was a Researcher with Chunghwa Telecom Co., Ltd., Taoyuan, Taiwan, from 1993 to 2001. His current research interests include Cloud Computing, Mobile Computing and Networks, Distributed Systems, and Fault-Tolerant Computing.

E-Mail: jwlin@csie.fju.edu.tw

1

The Internet of Things (IoT) Paradigm: The Use Cases

1.1 INTRODUCTION TO INTERNET OF THINGS

Internet of Things (IoT) is the interconnection of networks along with sensors for the transmission of recorded data from the environment to the user. It is stated that the innovations in IoT are accepted and it is evolving at a rapid speed, which helps in reducing the workforce and increasing the productivity in many real-time applications (Karthikeyan et al 2019). Industry professionals and academicians are continuously looking out for proper use, company, and scientific cases in order to assertively and clearly proclaim the transformational power of the IoT concept to the larger viewers of global end-users, engineers, executives, and entrepreneurs (Chan 2015). IoT architecture is given in Figure 1.1.

1.1.1 Digitized Entities

With the quicker firmness and development of edge and digitization technologies such as sensors, actuators, chips, controllers, tags, beacons, codes, stickers, LEDs, specks, smart dust, etc., all our electrical, mechanical, and physical systems become systematically digitized to join the mainstream computing. Additionally, these digitized items are integrated with cloud-related applications, services, and data sources in order to be adequately active and reactive. All sorts of digitized entities and elements individually as well as collectively are thus enabled to become active, sensitive, responsive, perceptive, receptive, communicative, and computational.

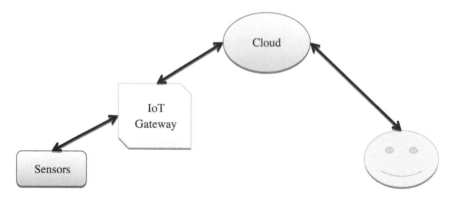

FIGURE 1.1
IoT architecture.

1.1.1.1 Connected Devices

Wearables devices, smart-phones, digital assistants, tablets manufacturing equipment, medical instruments, robots, drones and defense equipment, and home appliances are connected through communication and data transmission protocols. Also, these ground-level devices are getting linked up with remotely held applications and data sources in order to be sharp in their events and reactions.

1.1.1.2 Cloud Services

Infrastructure, platform, and software are the most familiar cloud services that are provided by the cloud service provider. In IoT, as the data are recorded continuously from the sensors, the recorded data will be stored in the cloud. Typically, the service depends upon the sensors and the user's requirements. If the user is using smart home appliances, then the user needs data storage and retrieval as a cloud service requirement (Yousefpour et al 2019). The flow in the cloud services is shown in Figure 1.2.

1.1.1.3 Edge/Fog Device Clouds

1.1.1.3.1 Edge Computing

It is the distributed computing, where it gets the IoT data closer to the user by using the edge devices.

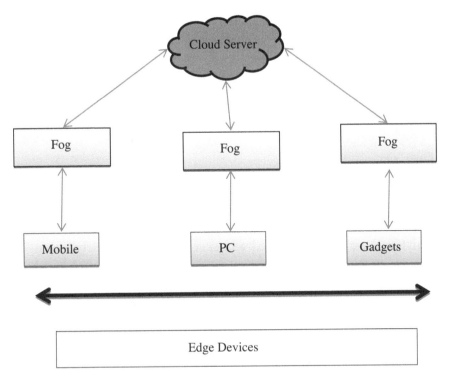

FIGURE 1.2
Cloud/Edge/Fog computing.

The two main objectives of edge computing are

1. Decrease in latency
2. Faster retrieval of data

Also, in order to eliminate the heterogeneity-induced complexities, containerization, micro services, container orchestration platforms, and service mesh solutions are collectively contributing immensely. Device-to-Device (D2D) integration frameworks, Device-to-Cloud (D2C) integration brokers, device middle-ware products, brokers, gateways, etc., are emerging in order to speed up the process of setting up and sustaining edge clouds. The main motivations for the unprecedented success of the edge cloud phenomenon are real-time data capture, processing, decision-making, and action.

1.1.1.3.2 Fog Computing

It is one of the decentralized computing where it acts as the intermediate layer between the cloud and the user environment. The recorded IoT data will be stored in the cloud as well as fog that enables the user to access the IoT data faster.

The two main objectives of fog computing are to

1. Increase the efficiency
2. Reduce the size of data to the cloud

1.1.2 IoT Analytics

The collaborations and correlations are bound to generate a lot of multi-structured and massive amount of data. With the steady arrival of path-breaking algorithms and analytics platforms, big and real-time data analytics are greatly simplified and speeded up. Data analytics are to extricate timely and actionable insights out of all sorts of IoT data. These acquired and aggregated insights can be looped back to IoT systems and applications in order to exhibit adaptive behavior (Raj and Lin 2019). That is, data-driven insights empower devices and software to behave in an intelligent fashion. As IoT data hides a variety of usable patterns, associations, tips, information, knowledge, etc., it is mandatory to collect every bit of IoT data with care and clarity.

1.1.3 IoT Applications

Thus, as the number of heterogeneous IoT devices is steadily growing, correspondingly the IoT data size is seeing an exponential growth. IoT applications are going to be hugely adaptive and adroit in their functions. Most of the IoT applications are to target and fulfill people empowerment. Individuals and innovators are going to be benefited immensely with all the advancements happening silently in the IoT space.

1.2 THE REASON WHY IoT IS STRATEGICALLY SOUND

1.2.1 IoT Leads to Smarter Computing

Cognition-enabled equipment and professional systems will become our casual and compact companions. Arrays of smarter systems will be bound to sustain us in our classrooms, homes, coffee shops, motels, offices, airports, gyms, and meeting points in big numbers. They will flawlessly attach, work together, and associate to understand mind, public and physical needs, and transport them in an extremely low-profile, safe, and relaxed style. It is nothing but the appropriate data, and correct services will be conceived, constructed, and sent to the required person at right time in the specified place.

1.2.2 IoT Delivers Smarter Environments

Packages, articles, and furnishings have become dominant by the computation and communication components by required electronics that are embedded into them (Neeba et al 2019).

1.2.3 IoT Prescribes the Shift toward People in IT

IT experts describe that there will be a huge and impulsive combination of daily technologies to make a technology cluster to accomplish society needs as well as professional requirements immediately. It is the place that gives the likelihood of the clear integration of minds with machines.

1.3 THE PROMINENT IoT REALIZATION TECHNOLOGIES

Many technologies are evolving every day, but only certain technologies are able to make an impact continuously. A few technologies have shown their strengths, providing innovation in business, transformation, and disruption.

- **Knowledge Engineering and Enhancement**
  Data are converted to information and then to transition of knowledge by using event processing engines, dissemination, processing, knowledge correlation, knowledge, analytics, and discovery data mining.
- **Interfacing**
  Natural, adaptive, intuitive, and informative interfaces
- **Real-time Insights**
  Through in-memory computing and in-database analytics, appliances are used for real-time processing of IoT big data (Feldman et al 2012).

- **Computing Paradigms**
  Paradigms such as mobile, autonomic, grid, social, service, on-demand, cloud, fog, and edge computing.
- **Digitization & Edge Technologies**
  LED, specks, implantable, wearable, portables beacons, chips, micro-controllers, tags, stickers, smart dust, motes, and invisible sensors (Raj and Raman 2015).
- **Sensing, Perception, and Vision**
  One of the most needed things for establishing IoT environment, i.e., miniaturization contains micro- and nano-scale electronics product.
- **Communication**
  Ambient, autonomic, and unified communication models providing standards-compliant 3G and other generation communication capabilities.
- **Context-Aware Computing**
  Vision, perception, ubiquitous sensing, and edge or fog clouds are considered to be context-aware computing.
- **Middleware Solutions**
  It consists of fusion, intermediate, arbitration, federation, enrichment, transformation, integration, and composition mechanism.
- **Compartmentalization through Virtualization and Containerization**
  One of the software engineering methods called divide and conquer is used on hardware to achieve flexibility and extensibility.

1.4 THE IoT: THE KEY APPLICATION DOMAINS

The applications of IoT are not limited to any single category, as it can implement in any form of appliances as per the requirement (Gubbi et al 2013). The end applications in all the developments in the IoT space area are intelligent workspaces and smarter environments such as smarter homes (Ferretti and Schiavone 2016).

The prominent components included in any IoT environment are electrical, mechanical, physical, and electronics embedded with smart labels, barcodes, LED lights, beacons, and pads (Bok 2016).

- **New Business Possibilities**
  The IoT-inspired era produces continuous and dominant force on industry and how it can run. The IoT idea improves business to

make streams for people, and response time will be faster to customer needs.

- **Trending toward the Insights as a Service (IaaS) Era**

  The data generation of IoT is high, and with the more rapid velocity and development of IoT data analytics products and platforms, the new service model of IaaS arises. Insights are available everywhere and constantly generated, which makes the data more reliable and stable.

- **Fresh Revenue Opportunities**

  The IoT can help companies ensure additional services on top of traditional lines of business by using the big data analytics as the previous data will help in that case.

Automation is at its peak. As with every tangible thing in an enterprise environment gets empowered and connected. There will be a fresh wave of compelling automation.

Regarding vendors there is no homogeneous IoT market, as every industry and IoT applications are different. With the irresistible cloud technology for quickly and easily achieving the long-standing goal of infrastructure optimization, the IT landscape with cloud achieved a crucial place.

IoT is a powerful and pioneering idea to be taken very seriously toward its implementation. The real difficulty is in the integration of heterogeneous systems and sensors. Additionally, it is important to extract insights from streaming data in all sources so that any decision can be made.

Knowledge engine is the right place that consists of an open and industry-strength integration container for impeccably differentiating all kinds of data analyzing, processing, mining, and then smartly disseminating the extracted knowledge to required person at right time.

1.5 IoT USE CASES

The subsequent sections describe the popular and prominent industry, consumer, and personal use cases out of all the distinct improvements and improvisations happening in the IoT space.

1.5.1 Smart Grids

It is a connected device that scales energy, water, or natural gas consumption of a building or home. Traditional meters scale total consumption, whereas smart meters scale time and how much of a resource is consumed. Power companies started to use smart grids due to the efficiency.

Smart metering also supports the following:

- Reducing operating expenses
- Improving forecasting
- Improving customer service
- Reducing energy theft

1.5.1.1 Optimizing the Power Grid

- General Electric has been touting the benefits of creating an "Electricity Value Network," in which digitization allows for visualization across the entire electricity system.

1.5.1.2 Smart Metering

- It covers smart meter data analytics, smart billing, meter networks, and smart energy profiling.

1.5.2 Smart Flights

The combination of Artificial Intelligence (AI) with IoT enables the passengers to get maximum benefits at minimum costs.

1.5.2.1 Imbuing Jet Engines with AI

- New C-Series jetliner boasted Pratt & Whitney's Geared Turbo Fan (GTF) engine and its 5000 sensors producing as much as 10 GB of data each second. It is shown in Figure 1.3.

1.5.3 Smart Agriculture and Farming

Predicting weather conditions such as rain, drought, snow, or wind helps farmers to handle these conditions before they occur. Greenhouse environment temperature and HVAC sensors permit control over microclimate conditions (Lee and Lee 2015).

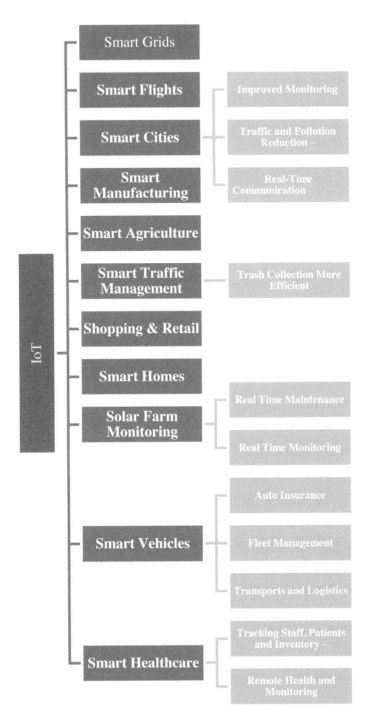

FIGURE 1.3
IoT use cases.

The benefits of smart agriculture are as follows:

- Growing Better Grapes for Better Vino
- Saving the Bees
- Using Drones to Save the Rainforest
- Plant and Soil Monitoring
- Livestock Monitoring
- Conservation Monitoring

1.5.3.1 Smart Farming

Farm resource savings using wireless sensors and remote monitoring devices

- Smart Tractors
- IoT-Based Pest Control

1.5.4 Smart Manufacturing

The Industrial Internet of Things (IIoT) utilizes both supply chain management and smart logistics.

1.5.5 Smart Cities

The IoT empowers Smart City, defined as a municipality that uses data and communication technologies to increase operational efficiency, share information, and enhance the quality of government services.

- Long search times for a parking space
- Exceeded emissions limits
- Illegal parking
- Valuable parking space not being monetized
- Costly yet ineffective parking space management systems

1.5.5.1 Real-Time Communication

The available parking space reduces the required time and distance to park, improving mobility. Overhead parking sensors mounted on lampposts connected through the IoT can analyze and measure the appropriate data, sending information to digital signage, ideally also integrated on the lamppost that can display the latest updates for drivers.

1.5.6 Traffic and Pollution Reduction

The decision to park right away in a nearby garage, rather than circling in the inner city to find an on-street parking space, is essential to avoid unnecessary emissions and traffic.

1.5.6.1 Improved Monitoring

Clever parking services and management solutions enable cities to automate processes that may be time-consuming or costly. These solutions allow users to identify trends and prioritize controls according to real occupancy and payment data. For example, the appropriate use of dedicated zones, such as handicap or delivery areas, can be continuously monitored. Safety in the city can be increased, and the identification of a hazard or non-authorized vehicles in certain zones can be easily established.

1.5.6.2 Smart Traffic Management

The traffic management implemented by IoT devices provides a Smart City initiative that can provide good decision-making and operations. IoT technology supports municipalities to make their cities more sustainable. Sensors will check air quality and urban noise in critical locations.

1.5.6.3 Making Trash Collection More Efficient

Urbiotica's M2M is a wireless autonomous sensor to tell whether trash bin is full or not. The information is sent to an Urbiotica that connects with systems to optimize trash-collection routes.

1.5.7 Shopping & Retail

The IoT can connect a user's mobile to a store window, help them finding what they need, and offer valuable information or special concessions for loyalty.

1.5.8 Smart Homes

Smart home sensors change the thermostat to modify temperature and turn off the lights if that room is not used by any individual.

1.5.9 Smart Healthcare

IoT rationalizes tracking of asset and enhances supply chain management. By using inventory management system, people can find essential tools rapidly.

1.5.9.1 Remote Health Monitoring

In certain situations, patients need not to go to an emergency room. Remote health monitoring is the most popular healthcare applications.

1.5.9.2 Ensuring the Availability and Accessibility of Critical Hardware

Many hospitals need next-gen software and hardware to operate, as many of these are used to save and prolong human life.

1.5.9.3 Healthcare

Electronic Medical Records (EMR) are used to analyze the patient's behavior by Machine Learning (ML) algorithm. Healthcare companies are streaming EMR data and using ML to predict the health of the patients (Suresh et al 2020).

1.5.10 Smart Vehicles

1.5.10.1 Using Sensors to Make Driving Safer

Companies developed technology that has sensors built into smart-phones to determine driver behavior. When data are collected, the app can give training to drive safer.

1.5.10.2 Transports and Logistics

Transportation and logistics require many data as possible for accurate and error-free management.

- Connected Car Systems Monitoring
- Real-Time Fleet Management
- Driver Safety Systems
- Smart Driving

There are many advantages of self-driving cars. It includes

- Overall reduction of vehicles.
- Driverless taxis

1.5.11 IoT-Enabled Telematics Use Cases

1.5.11.1 Fleet Management

Fleet management reduce the risks associated by improving efficiency and productivity for the companies that largely rely on transport.

1.5.11.2 Auto Insurance

Drivers can install Official Equipment Manufacturer device to check driving behaviors. It allows for auto insurance agencies to best price coverage applicable for the driver.

1.5.11.3 Transit Fleets (Mobility-as-a-Service)

The respected services depend upon the user to use the asset responsibly as they move from one location to other location.

1.5.11.4 The Beneficiaries of the Telematics Use Cases

It includes

- Rental car companies
- Shipping and delivery companies

- Utility companies
- Sensors-inspired smart parking

1.5.12 Solar Farm Monitoring & Analytics Using Cloud IoT Core

1.5.12.1 Real-Time Monitoring

Solar farms are typically metered as a total output of a few arrays.

1.5.12.2 Real-Time Maintenance

Farm manager will get notifications of every panel instead of than trying to guess about the performance associated with it.

1.5.13 IoT Use Cases in Marketing/Sales

The following are the scenarios where IoT are used in large scale.

- Customer Insights and Opportunities
- Flexible Billing and Pricing Models
- New Value-Added Services

1.5.14 IoT Use Cases in Product Development

The following are the scenarios where IoT are used on a large scale of product development.

- **Connected Product Quality Analysis**
  Root-cause analysis improvement and right steps to give good quality, safety, and reliability
- **Connected Software Management**
  Identification of remote areas, product configuration management, and control

1.5.15 IoT Use Cases in Operations/Manufacturing

The following are the scenarios where IoT are used on a large scale.

- Asset and Material Tracking
- Industrial Automation

- Connected Operations Intelligence
- Unified Key Performance Indicators
- Real-Time Asset Health Monitoring
- Operations Management Improvements

1.5.16 IoT Use Cases in Education

The following are the scenarios where IoT are used on a large scale.

- Mobile Learning
- School Security
- Building Automation

1.5.17 IoT Use Cases for the Oil and Gas Industry

The following are the scenarios where IoT are used on a large scale.

1.5.17.1 Redefining Field-Based Intel for the Oil and Gas Industry

Oil and gas customers can optimize placement of drill heads in real time to optimize output of the well thereby increasing productivity and revenue.

1.5.18 Physical Security Use Cases

The following are the scenarios where IoT are used on a large scale.

1.5.18.1 Improving Physical Security

Consider a man in a ski mask outside of a bank couldn't even get through the door because the camera identified the activity as suspicious and consequently told the doors to lock, the alarms to sound and the police to come. That is the level of increased security that our AI-driven, video-centric IoT technology can provide – the ability to assess a security threat, act on it, and ultimately prevent crime.

1.5.19 Optimization Use Cases

The following are the scenario where IoT are used on a large scale.

1.5.19.1 Business Optimization

Consider one store where nobody required waiting in line. You simply walk in, take the products you want, and walk out. This can be accomplished through a combination of computer vision, deep learning algorithms, and sensor fusion that would allow customers to be identified and charged conveniently behind the scenes.

1.5.20 IoT Edge Data Analytics Use Cases

The following are the scenarios where IoT are used on a large scale.

1.5.20.1 Thwarting Illegal Fishing

In order to limit illegal fishing practices, the Port of New Bedford installed Dell Edge Gateways, with V5 Systems solar video surveillance technologies to better track person coming in and out of the port.

- Smart Appliances
- Water Treatment
- Fire and Safety
- Smart Plug

1.5.21 IoT Use Cases for Business

The following are the scenarios where IoT are used on a large scale.

1.5.21.1 Smart Lighting

The optimal space illumination ensuring invaluable security.

1.5.21.2 Security and Access Controls

It makes detection of intruders much easier and access management of users.

1.5.22 IoT Use Case in Consumer Electronics

1.5.22.1 Smart House/Smart Office

Achieving building automation through use of connected devices

1.5.23 IoT Use Cases in Logistics

1.5.23.1 Smart Labels

Real-time inventory tracking by speeding up warehouse operations

1.5.23.2 Cargo Integrity Monitoring

Integrating electronics in containers and tracking cargo in its route

1.5.23.3 Consumer Product Usage Analysis for Marketing

The IoT possesses the potential to completely change the way businesses deal with customers.

1.5.23.4 Serving Consumers and Business Users with the Same Analytics

Analytics on IoT data is important because it attains both business-facing and consumer-facing.

1.5.23.5 Sensors and Cameras Enable Connected Events

Social analytics involves use sensor data, video data, and social media data to get actionable insights individuals as well as groups.

1.5.23.6 Video Analytics for Surveillance and Safety

Infrastructure protection goes beyond predictive maintenance.

1.5.23.7 Predictive Maintenance

Keeping assets up and running has the potential to significantly decrease operational expenditures.

1.5.23.8 Asset Tracking

The asset tracking objective is to permit an enterprise to easily locate and monitor key assets, including along the supply chain (e.g. raw materials,

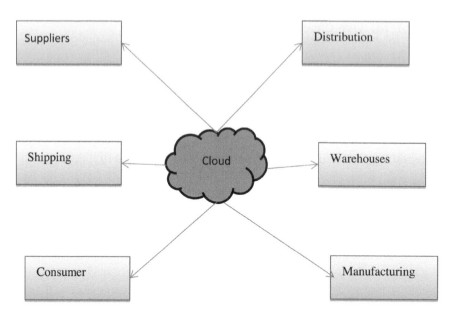

FIGURE 1.4
Cloud appliances.

final products and containers) to optimize logistics, maintain inventory levels, prevent quality issues, and detect a theft.

1.6 AN INTEGRATED AND INSIGHTS-DRIVEN IoT APPLICATION SCENARIO

Cloud Service Brokerage (CSB) establishes connection among many cloud service providers. The cloud occupies the prime spot in any integrated environment. CSB streamlines and simplifies the complex integration hurdles and hitches as shown in Figure 1.4.

1.7 CONCLUSION

The connection between AI and IoT may not be immediately obvious, but the two work and help people in their needs. On one hand, IoT sensors let AI systems experience their environment directly. On the other hand, and machine learning achieve glean actionable insights from the vast arrays of IoT devices spewing out more data than humans can easily make sense of environment. The IoT applications are practically limitless, and many applications are being developed all the time. Along with the incredible opportunity, some challenges in optimizing a technology that reaches deeply into so many aspects of our businesses and our lives.

2

An Intelligent IoT Framework for Smart Water Management in Agriculture

2.1 INTRODUCTION TO ARCHITECTURE OF SMART AGRICULTURE

The biggest challenges in agricultural productivity are to subdue variability, where farmers must understand about the characteristics of the field and the improvement of the crops. This can be finished through precision agriculture that envisions a deeper agricultural record capturing, thus accumulating information in every step from planning to final product, within the agricultural manufacturing method. Furthermore, precision agriculture systems can assist farmers with selection making and aid control while integrating different data sources consisting of sensors, satellites, and meteorologist forecasts.

Traditional strategies of agriculture used by farmers have become out of date and ineffective. So in order to reach their goals, farmers are introducing those new records structures in their farms. Through preserving a repository of sensed facts, it becomes feasible to research the field's behavior, helping the farmer to attain the intention of better use of sources, lowering the costs of production, and ensuring food safety. However, in the agricultural manufacturing manner, there's a widespread quantity of entities, everybody producing statistics. This is required to be captured. The arrival of precision agriculture introduced new assets of data at farmer's disposal, which enabled the growth of their farm's productivity. To further improve the reduction of production charges, it's much necessary to accumulate new varieties of information like what's happening in each step of the production method. For large-scale farms, it is now possible to clear up the problem of automatic facts acquisition, using Global Positioning

System (GPS), satellite imagery, and superior sensors, all presenting records to specialized software program, capable of studying and relating data. The established solutions are modified to mechanized, industrialized methods and they are not applicable to small-scale agriculture or unable to stop information in every method steps. It is also said few farms with unique crops (vegetables, fruits, and plants) in which no huge machines are used, the farmers need to use manual exertions within the production method. In these kinds of plants, there may be a loss of systems that are able to automate the procedure of dealing with the employee conduct which, as said before, maybe useful to provide higher information approximately about the crops and the field when incorporated with other assets of statistics.

Yahyaoui et al (2017) anticipated the concept of monitoring workers' movements in a winery with tagged equipment to reveal the workers' activities. Contreras et al (2017) advanced a wearable module for recording the worker's positioning in orchards, emphasizing the importance of getting such structures become a fashionable agricultural trend to triumph over the agricultural employee–monitoring trouble. There's a need to create answers capable of tracking the behavior of each character and equipment to combine statistics from specific employees, the usage of awesome area systems with different resources of data given by several sensors present within the discipline. New machine will be able to monitor agricultural workforces, which is important, thus maintaining a registry of the events occurring throughout crop's lifecycle. This chapter depicts the challenges to overcome while developing a monitoring and collecting data system focused on agriculture.

In unique crop farms, in which they use much less employee with mechanized production methods, it is hard to extract the agricultural process information. Then, the necessity of human labor for their farms makes the technique of data collection complicated. Among other difficulties that are accompanied with specialty crops is the availability of perennial crops of trees or vines. In agricultural subject, communication and electricity are great assets, whereas precision agricultural structures can be power green or modified according to different resources of power in the solar cells.

An agricultural workforce's device must not impact the worker's productivity. It must be definitely embedded with activities of employee, but should not disturb their overall performance and the farmers desire a statistics granularity and detect issues of -person plant (Jayalakshmi and Gomathi 2019).

It is intended to create a system able to accumulate location data records about transferring agricultural workers on the field. The variety of activities that farmers perform throughout a season is large, focusing on a single rural manufacturing method, with the intention of harvesting. The delicate nature of strong plants generally requires farmers to harvest their vegetation with human workforces compared to mechanized systems. It is necessary to be aware of all agricultural events and choosing the activities that occur around places and also maintaining a registry about the work being executed in the course of the field. These days, smartphones are becoming less expensive and are enabled with vicinity recognition technologies. So, the result may be achieved by using smartphones; however, it can give the options to apply different gadgets.

In a human-monitoring method, the purpose to seize productiveness metrics is vital and it is essential that the farmers overall performance is not affected either with the solution or the production manner. In this scenario, the framework should be implemented to special human bodies based on gender, weight and height so that you can monitor every farmer who works in a farm without their overall efficiency being affected. In case of agricultural process, farmers need to realize metrics together with the harvested fruit weight in line with tree or maybe the range of orchards in which the farmers carried out the activity that was supposed to occur.

2.2 CASE STUDY

Agricultural and water management activities vary according to the crop that is monitored. Olive production is chosen to assess the method of making smarter water management in precision agriculture. This way of life was selected compared to other ones due to the convenience of access to olive orchards and heterogeneity of tree sizes and displacement between distinctive orchards, which facilitates while comparing the system for actual use cases (Kumar et al 2015).

This crop will allow assessing performances on agricultural employee–monitoring systems and evaluating the technique of creating such gadgets. Olive oil being the principle derived manufactured from olive crop, its market desires to identify and decrease manufacturing costs, searching for metrics in each manufacturing phases from tree pruning to olives harvesting (Li et al 2015).

Measuring the expenses allows one an evaluation of the average price among specific production strategies (Li et al 2015).Traditional olive orchards have an average distance of 10-12 m between trees, with an average plant density of 80 to 120 trees/Ha (Venkatesh et al 2015).

In the case of non-mechanizable olive orchards, they are usually installed on hillsides with inclinations greater than 20%, limiting them to that cultivation system. On the other hand, intensive and super-intensive olive orchards have higher plant densities with 200 to 600 trees/Ha and 1000 to 2000 trees/Ha, respectively.

In super-intensive olive orchards, harvesting is done by machines, specialized for specific olive tree cultivars. The distance between rows is about 6 minutes an intensive orchard and it decreases to 4 minutes super-intensive orchards. Those high-density olive orchards are typically irrigated, achieving productive yields of about 8,000 to 12,000 kg/Ha.

2.3 WORKFORCE MONITORING CHALLENGES

Agricultural worker's monitoring is one of the major areas of precision agriculture in the scientific research. This section presents the challenges to overcome while developing a monitoring system focused on agriculture (Singh et al 2015).

In specialty crop farms, where mechanized production processes is less used, it is difficult to extract the agricultural process data. The need to use human labor in such farms makes the process of data capturing more complex, making it a human-monitoring problem.

Another problem related to specialty crops is the presence of perennial crops such as trees or vines. Trees are a major issue to wireless communication systems, which may cause signal attenuation.

In the agricultural field, communication and energy are available as scarce resources; therefore, precision agricultural systems must be energy efficient.

A system detecting agricultural workforces might not influence the worker's productivity. It must be integrated with worker activities, not interfering in their performance or comfort.

Specialty crops have an inherent low tolerance to errors while tracking the location where specific agricultural activities take place. In these types of crops, the farmer needs to have a granularity of data so that they can detect problems in an individual plant.

2.4 RELATED WORK

Major approaches to find the traceability issue must be tested by using barcodes, Radio Frequency Identification (RFID), GPS, and few mobile solutions. Venkatesh et al (2015) developed a system to generate yield maps of hand-harvested fruit using a GPS recorder, by marking large containers with their fruit picking locations.

Li et al (2015) developed a wearable module to check positions of employee, applied to orchards or cultivation environments which are protected, in which GPS signal is not available. The method focuses on finding the relative and absolute position location systems by farming workers.

In spite of capturing the employees' positioning, worker-monitoring systems must have the potential to differentiate between human activities done in the crop such as pruning, spraying, and harvesting, and activities such as standing still or walking. Hence, it is required to get other method than those that are applied in large-scale mechanized agriculture and it should categorize from other solutions that only check production crops.

2.5 NOVEL TECHNIQUE FOR SMART WATER MANAGEMENT IN PRECISION AGRICULTURE

Water irrigation control is one of the typical usages of computer systems in agriculture. Water is a useful resource with predominant impact to farmer's fulfilment, impacting manufacturing costs without delay. Farmers employ computer devices to enable water automation and control, to enhance water intake, to provide warnings when soil humidity reaches high, and to perform variable rate irrigation.

Irrigation management systems are typically based on Wireless Sensor Networks (WSNs) and Internet of Things, and provide user interface to show information about field water resources, to the agriculture expert (Kumar et al 2015). The proposed system was intended to demonstrate as to how an automatic irrigation system can be used to reduce water consumption. Each network node was composed of both temperature and soil-moisture sensors, a radio modem ZigBee, rechargeable batteries, and a photovoltaic cell (Li et al 2015).

These nodes were deployed at ground level, near the plant roots, in order to measure soil moisture and temperature levels. A gateway is used to automate the activation of irrigation when the thresholds of moisture and temperature are reached. It is also used to communicate with the sensor nodes using ZigBee and with the remote server using mobile cellular data network, based on GPRS and GSM (Li et al 2015). A solution for this problem is the use of a memory card to store data locally to the gateway. An overview of system is presented in Figure 2.1 and it is representative of the general irrigation systems used in precision agriculture.

The implementation of the described system was deployed to a sage crop and allowed a water usage optimization with 60 and 90% savings compared to a traditional water irrigation system in the performed experiments. Venkatesh et al (2015) developed a wireless smart sensor array for

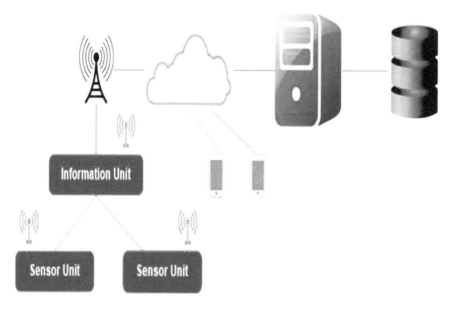

FIGURE 2.1
An overview of system employing WSNs.

irrigation scheduling in cotton crop. This system is composed of sensors (moisture sensors and thermocouples), electronics board, RFID tags, and a laptop computer with two antennas attached.

However, in this scenario, it applied the method to reduce the automatic irrigation cost and scheduling employing off-the-shelf components, while still improving irrigation performance. To attain the referred goal, RFID tags are used for transmission of data to the central node, for example, laptop with antennas. Another solution needed the licenses uses for radio frequency, where using RFID tags transmission, at 2.4GHz, which does not need licensing, leads to a reduction of cost. The disadvantage of the 2.4GHz frequency is that sometimes wireless transmission can be broken during data communication.

The environmental plants create a major blow on the wireless transmitters and they are required to be located higher than the plants' top so that they can avoid signal attenuation. The smart sensor boards are power-driven with a 9V battery that has the potential to give power throughout the crop's growing season fully, doing sensor measurements and data transmission every hour in that time period. In order to be more precise, irrigate the field using water only where it is really needed, which is also known as variable-rate irrigation.

When using this irrigation method, data about both soil and atmosphere parameters like moisture, temperature, and humidity are needed. In order to do irrigation (Venkatesh et al 2015), it needs five in-field sensing stations to be mounted across the field, periodically sending local sensed information a base station computer. With distance, data rate, compatibility, and cost in mind, it is decided to make use of the Bluetooth protocol to perform communications between the sensing stations and the base station machine, leaving behind ZigBee and other license-free radio frequency transmission protocols.

Field sensor scanning was made every 10 seconds and transmission to the base station was made every 15 minutes. Because Bluetooth is a heavy power consuming protocol, the Bluetooth modules were draining the sensing station batteries every 3–5 days, even with solar-powered recharging. To solve this problem, it is needed to develop a hardware power-saving module to force the modules into sleep mode. With the help of a photovoltaic cell, the system was able to keep the batteries charged and maintaining the required 5V electric tension. Interference from the biomass was noted during deployment forcing them to raise the transmitting modules from 50 to 150 cm height. The irrigation machine had a GPS sensor installed and it oversaw sending the sprinkler location to the base station.

This information combined with the data from the sensing station enabled the base station machine to inform to the irrigation machine which sprinklers needed to be on and off at any given point in time. In order to augment the control of the whole system by end-users, a user-friendly decision-making interface was developed, enabling adjustments for each sprinkler, based on the sensed data. This project proved the feasibility of a precise site-specific irrigation system, with low-cost, off-the-shelf equipment, and remote operation of field machinery.

To scale irrigation production efficiency between drip and sprinkler irrigation systems on these vegetables, data were manipulated, in which production efficiency (%) can be detected as a response variable:

$$\text{Production efficiency (\%)} = \frac{\text{Total output (N)}}{\text{Total input costs used in the production}} * 100$$

The production efficiency is compared between the two irrigation systems such as drip and sprinkler, and every crop will be analyzed separately.

In general, more production input costs are used on crops production under drip irrigation compared to the sprinkler irrigation, in which drip farmers spend more on water and fertilizer and their production efficiency is comparably high on all the vegetables, which do not contain much difference in the observation.

To summarize in drip irrigation, expenses are huge in production inputs, still their efficiency of production is much high to sprinkler irrigation in all three vegetable crops.

2.6 MACHINE LEARNING TECHNIQUE FOR SMARTER AGRICULTURE

Machine learning algorithms contain three different categories such as:

- Learning
- Validation and
- Classification (Ali and Smith 2006)

The initial phase is where any algorithm finds to categorize the data points by making a knowledge model with the appropriate features of data. Machine learning is a specialization of computer and an expeditiously trending topic in context, and is anticipated to bang more (Suresh et al 2020).

2.6.1 Feature Selection Applications

- Abbreviating the measurement cost and accommodation requirements
- Minimizing exploitation and training time
- Promoting data understanding and data conception (Ali and Smith 2006)

Here, it is necessary to understand the information and note the observation for the society. Evaluating data manually is not feasible in few places, takes time, and disturbs productivity (Suresh et al 2020).

There are two types of data used in machine learning.

1. Labeled data
2. Unlabeled data

2.6.2 Labeled Data

In labeled data, the attributes are essential so that they could imply a tag to the information used in supervised learning (Suresh et al 2020).

2.6.3 Unlabeled Data

Unlabeled data are implemented in unsupervised learning as they contain only data points (Suresh et al 2020).

2.6.4 Supervised Learning

Supervised learning does learning map by the variables X and Y, input, and output variables. This makes output for invisible data.

There are further two types of classification in supervised learning.

1. Regression
2. Classification

A regression could be used within certain variables for a statistical relationship among two or more variables. Classification arises very commonly in day-to-day life. Substantially, it contains partitioning up the objects. Each object is accredited to one of several mutually exhaustive and exclusive kinds known as classes. Every object must authorize to only one class (Suresh et al 2020).

2.7 DIMENSION REDUCTION TECHNIQUES

This reduction is just the procedure of declining the number of random variables of the input without harming any sort of information. Larger amounts of input variables and bigger data samples result in an increase of intricacy of the dataset. In order to reduce the memory and statistical time, the dimensionality of dataset is decreased. This decrease also supports to terminate needless input variables like replication of variables or variables with a truncated significance level (Jayalakshmi and Gomathi 2019).

These reduction techniques are:

1. Feature Extraction
2. Feature Selection

This framework is comprised of two parts, utilization of search engine and obtaining the best candidate from the given criteria. The filter method can be used for the classifier while a wrapper method uses a classifier to measure subsets.

Filtering methods such as bilateral information, autonomous component analysis, class detaching measure, or variable ranking could be effectively used for the classification. By combining several features, these methods transform the feature set into a lower-dimensional feature vector. Extraneous and redundant features are discarded by supervised feature selection that arbitrates relevant features by their affiliation with the corresponding class labels (Suresh et al 2020).

In this selection, k dimensions are chosen away from d dimensions that provide much information and reject the $(d\text{-}k)$ dimensions. In addition, this selection is also termed as the subset selection. The best subset consists

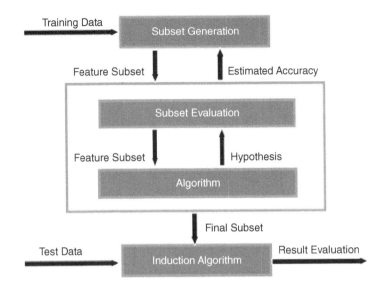

FIGURE 2.2
Feature selection.

of few amounts of dimensions that devote the majority to the accuracy. The finest subset is set up with an appropriate error function.

Training the data is placed all the way through a definite process of subset production which is shown in Figure 2.2, for instance, sequential backward selection. The subsequent set is now placed through a procedure to test its performance. If this performance endures the anticipated conditions, then it will be designated as the final subset. Or else, the deriving subset will once more be placed through the procedure of subset generation for more fine-tuning.

Feature selection has two different approaches: sequential forward selection and backward selection.

2.8 SEQUENTIAL FORWARD SELECTION

This selection commences a representation which doesn't consist of any predictors, and thereby the predictors are computed with the model, individually till the last predictors. In exacting, at each measurement the variable which provides the maximum supplementary enhancement to the fit is included to the model. Let us indicate a set by *P*, which contains the variables Xi, $i = 1,......,d$ and $E(P)$ is the error provoked in the test sample.

2.9 RANDOM FOREST

This is known as a classifier that composed of an accumulation of decision trees, where every tree is built by employing an algorithm A on the training set S and an extra arbitrary vector, individually as well as equivalently appropriated from a certain allocation. The estimation of the random forest is evolved by a maximum vote over the estimations of each tree.

The algorithm of the Random Forest functions by the given procedure:

1. Selects indiscriminate *K* data points from the guided data.
2. Assembles a decision tree for those particular *K* data points.
3. Accepts the Ntree subset and acts upon step 1 and step 2.
4. Determines the division or concludes on the behalf of the superiority of votes.

2.10 NAÏVE BAYES

This classifier classifies by using Bayes theorem to categorize the data. This accepts the probability of definite feature X is entirely solitary of the other feature Y.

2.10.1 Classification of Naïve Bayes

1. Multinomial Naïve Bayes
2. Gaussian Naïve Bayes
3. Bernoulli Naïve Bayes

Multinomial Naïve Bayes is implemented in multinomial distributed data, Gaussian Naïve Bayes is used in the classification problems, and

Bernoulli Naïve Bayes is implemented in data with multivariate Bernoulli distribution.

Generating a perceptron usually starts by conveying random weights. Every input is taken individually and multiplied by its weight. The generation of the output takes place by transferring the sum throughout an activation function. If it is a simple binary output, then activation function tells whether the perceptron is to be "fired" or not. For instance, if the sum is positive number, then 1 will be the output; if the sum is negative, then −1 will be the output. Additional factor to be considered is bias. If both the inputs are equal to zero, then any sum would be zero which is independent of multiplicative weight. To end this problem, a third input is summed which is called as the bias input with a value of 1.

To train the perceptron, subsequent steps are followed:

1. Afford the perceptron with inputs which have a well-known respond.
2. Inquire the perceptron to deduce a respond.
3. Calculate the error.
4. Regulate all the weights with the error, and then go to step 1 and do again.

This process repeated until getting the satisfied error. This is the way a single perceptron would function. Then, link all the perceptron in layers in the input and in the output, in order to produce a neural network (Krauss et al 2017). The layers amid the input and the output will be hidden layers.

Due to this methodology, neural network are called a feed-forward network. In the current scenario, it uses the backward propagation that comes under the concept of supervised neural networks. The correction factor could be denoted in the form of Δaij for the weights aij, similar to the least mean square algorithm that is equal to $\partial \epsilon k / \partial aij(k)$, which denotes the sensitivity factor that could be always negative. The correction factor is written by Eq. 2.1 (Suresh et al 2020),

$$aij(k+1) = aij(k) + uk\,\Delta aij(k) + bk\,\Delta aij(k-1) \qquad (2.1)$$

Where *uk* denotes the coefficient of learning factor and
bk Δaij(k-1) is said to be the momentum term.

The concept of self-organization comes under the category of unsupervised learning where the training data could be utilized for detecting

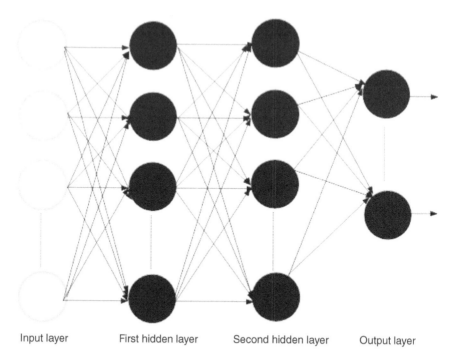

Input layer   First hidden layer   Second hidden layer   Output layer

FIGURE 2.3
Two-dimensional neural network model.

the clusters. The internal parameters within the input are compared with the feature map elements and the element that fits into the best match could be the victor. This successful element is taken into consideration and it should be trained further so that these data could be well used and responsive for the accessed input. Kohonen self-organizing feature maps are a supplementary evolvement of the competitive learning. In this case, the best corresponding elements will make their relative element to take part in their training set.

The two-dimensional neural network layer is shown in Figure 2.3.

This process leads to the similarity of the adjacent elements. In this situation, the analogous characteristics elements could form themselves as a cluster that maps each other and that set that forms as a feature map, could be considered as a two-dimensional data set. The self-organizing Kohonen neural network feature map is shown in Figure 2.4, which consists of two input layers that are bounded to each and every feature of the output layer.

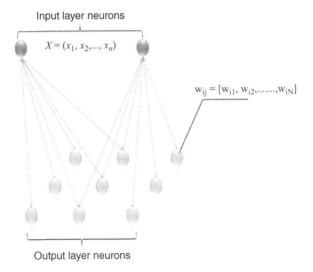

FIGURE 2.4
Kohonen self-organizing feature map.

The functionality of the self-organizing map could be denoted by the weights that are initialized to the random variables and the ith mapping element that could vary from $k=0$, 1, 2, 3,........., y is given in Equation 2.2.

$$\| c(k) - ac\,(k) \| = \min\{\| c(k) - wi(k) \|\} \qquad (2.2)$$

Where, c denotes the best matching pair.

During the past years, neural network-integrated with the fuzzy logic combination has been used widely in varieties of application. The natural integration procedure follows both the hybrid neural network with the fuzzy-based systems rather than using a traditional system. They have certain universal and harmonizing activities in common.

2.11 SPECIFICATION

The objective of artificial neural network is to detect the abnormal condition and worsening of a mechanical behavior of the equipment. In detecting these habits, the machines must be trained. This detection must be declared at a first sign itself, since the machine could provide the same vibration sign as before that could give a false pattern of the malfunction. Hence, the most enough mechanical faults should be evaluated at the first itself. At this scenario, the inherent capacity of the generalized neural network could be more suitable. The fault identification could be done by inserting certain malfunction dataset into the trained neural network model that could result in the fault classification pattern.

For instance, the dataset of the first and second harmonics of the vibrational data could be fed to the machines. If the first harmonic exists in the machine, then the value of imbalance and the probability of misaligned could be detected.

Further, if the second harmonics exists then, again, a value of misalignment and imbalance could be produced which could be analyzed by the neural network.

2.12 DESIGN

This is completely regarding the monitoring of the machine. Suppose if any vibrational sensor has been fit into the machine, then these data must be validated. This could be done by the data acquisition system. The data acquisition system is nothing but a board that could convert the analogy values coming from the transmitter into a digital format. It could be monitored with 256 channels that could relate to eight machines. This could generate the alarm data when certain abnormal circumstances occur. This could be indicated with the alarm system that could be fitted with the equipment, else it could be indicated with the certain LED (Light Emitting Diode) lights.

Typical performing situation or run-out spectra may be chosen and operational parameters data. Certain operation could be done by the online processing module:

1. The Root Mean Square (RMS) value could be estimated for the vibrational signals, since these data should be compared with the predefined limits of upper and lower values. Unless the RMS value works at a normal condition, the indication of the led could be normal.

2. In any situation if the RMS value has crossed its limit line, there could be an indication, say any alarm sound or indication of different LED light. If it retains its normal limit then no problem occurs, the system could regain its normal position as mentioned in point 1. After a certain interval of time if the RMS value continues to cross its limit condition, then there occurs the occurrence of vibration spectrum and this could be indicated and recorded. Then, when the limit value is adjusted, the system starts to regain its normal condition. A different LED light helps us to analyze different scenarios of the equipment.

3. This could be continued several times of a day and the values obtained by the vibration sensors, RMS values should be necessarily recorded and stored in the hard disk, which could be used as the reference later.

2.13 METHODOLOGY

It is necessary to validate the sensor data properly in the form of time and frequency domain. An important point to be noted is that the supervised learning methodology that comes with the study of vibrational data is not real-time operating data. The features of a good sensor input data, which are obtained from its normal working condition, should be necessarily considered. Under the normal condition, the working of the sensor is obtained so that the appropriate processing flags the potential malfunction modes and the widespread processing points to the most possible fault and its origin. For this, a fuzzy-based system is best suitable to get in reach with the family of sensors.

By using the support of trend analysis, it can determine the maximum risk factors that could occur in the machines of the industry. For this evaluation, it could use certain measurement dataset concerning to the measured points of the machine. With the help of regression curves, it could able to infer the particular operating system the alarm is going to be reached. These set of variables could be predefined by the operators.

Predictive maintenance will be effectual if interpretation regarding the vibration development beside the time is accomplished. Prediction is the difficulty of drawing calculations regarding known time series into the future. Hybrid neural network is nothing but a combination of fuzzy logic system that could be helpful in making a certain decision.

2.13.1 Fuzzy-Based Decision System

The fuzzy system is helpful for making certain sort of decision-making. It uses the normal IF-THEN statement for its decision. The combination of fuzzy system in the artificial neural network helps us in providing a crisp output. The input data determined by the machines could be evaluated through the fuzzy logic system to produce a crisp input. This in turn combines with certain decision-making statement and filters out itself with the logical and necessary data. These filtered fuzzy data are sent to the process of Defuzzification, where the fuzzy input data produce themselves to become crisp output data. The block diagram of this process is shown in Figure 2.5.

Human activity–detection systems can be used if needed to observe a few characteristics of everyday public behavior. Those systems make use of sensors installed near the user's body and detect what activity is being performed at a given time. There is smartphone or wearable powered systems that can inform if a sports person is on foot or running based on his movements. But, here farming employee monitoring and monitored actions can be chosen depending on the agricultural production methods.

The current solutions that are available in precision agriculture are restricted to the activities that machines perform in the land. Changing to labor-monitoring systems, it has no activity detection phase, making decision when agricultural work is done exactly to a human. With the

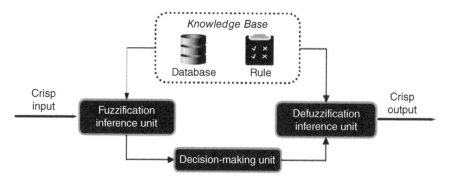

FIGURE 2.5
Block diagram for the fuzzy logic system.

goal to enrich the information available to farmers about their crops and production processes, here it proposes an agricultural activity-detection system for specialty crop workers. This tool also makes it to achieve farmers to check the worker's productivity, a common method that is familiar in agriculture; still, it is mostly based on less objective information.

2.14 RESULTS

Applications can detect environment by using gyroscope, accelerometer, and magnetometer in a smartphone. Every sensor will have three axes adding for a total of nine data points captured at a period of 0.02 seconds. The major way is to detect inertial data points at a period of 0.02-seconds, manually annotating data with the respected activities that were made. Since each data point has no means to relate to another one, it is needed to create a solution to relate small sets of data points that correspond to the execution of an activity. To solve this problem, dynamic sliding window that aggregates points of physic activity data to feed the classification algorithms.

The solution implements a sliding window algorithm that will apply to the data points of each of the smartphone sensors (accelerometer, magnetometer, and gyroscope). The algorithm starts by reading a total of 150 data points to an array. Each data point has nine points of data, one for each sensor axis. The algorithm calculates the 45 features using the set if statistics previously mentioned one for each axis of each sensor.

The method is to divide the problem in two monitoring tasks:

- Worker location detection
- Worker activity monitoring

The location process corresponds to the process of tracking worker's positioning is shown in Figure 2.6. The worker's location is not representative of the work they do in the whole day; so, it is necessary for a human activity–detection system to take place. The initial phase needs the worker to go head a previously known distance. A human step makes a peak which is more than $13 m/s^2$. Considering this into account, it shows a $12 m/s^2$ threshold that ignores small worker movements.

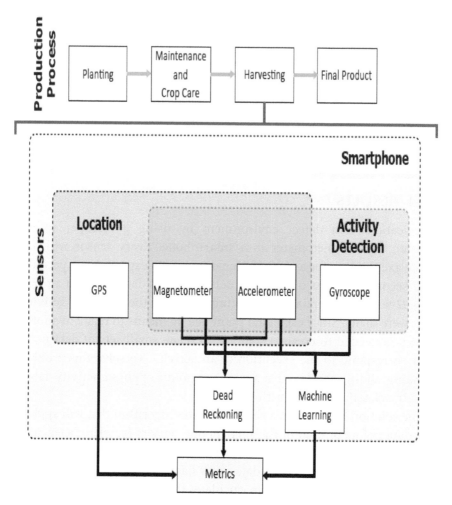

FIGURE 2.6
Location process.

These systems make use of sensors installed near the user's body and detect what activity is being performed at a given time. From the list of classifiers that were adapted to the type of data captured with the smartphone sensors, the ones with better performance were Bayes Net that implement a Bayes Network and the Multilayer Perceptron, which is based on Neural Networks. When comparing these two algorithms, it is observed that the Bayes Network is faster to create the classification models than Multilayer Perceptron, a known disadvantage of Neural Network algorithms.

2.15 CONCLUSION

This chapter started by studying the state of the art of precision agriculture and search for opportunities to improve in its various areas. It is found that most systems are focused on big, large-scale farms where there is a large investment on new sensors and machinery. To feed the agricultural models, new data need to be captured in all the agricultural production process steps, including the activities that in smaller or less mechanized farms need to be done by hand. The need for a global understating about what is happening with the crop at every moment led farmers to install new technology in their fields that monitor soil, weather, and pests during crop's life cycle. Other farmers have the activities held in the field monitored by capturing machinery location and productivity data. The available solutions are usually not adapted to smaller farms or those with specialty crops where a large percentage of the work is done by hand. To improve the knowledge that farmers have on their farms, an agricultural worker–monitoring system has been introduced that is capable to identify human labor in a rural environment.

3

IoT-Enabled Smart Traffic Control System for Congestion Control

3.1 A BRIEF INTRODUCTION TO ARCHITECTURE OF SMART TRAFFIC

The applications of IoT in traffic management are violation monitoring, non-stop electronic highways, and security systems (Omina 2015). The ubiquitous IoT in transport management gives Ubiquitous Transport Systems (UTS), which possess Intelligent Transport Management Systems (ITMSs) and UbiComp. The ITMS is used to monitor the environments. The scaling can be done from the delay time estimation; delay is the extra duration a driver takes to travel over a road.

If UTS is to be utilized properly, it must possess different characteristics criteria described in Figure 3.1 (Omina 2015).

It includes

1. Transportation services at all point of places and all time
2. Data must be environment-dependent and
3. Data are device-independent

The interactions are transparent and the UTS has real-time services.

The ubiquitous arrangement of road makes it challenging in implementing the methodology, here, text and audio are utilized. This component takes into consideration the acquisition of the most recent road status, consequently making it conceivable to discover elective courses. The exceptional element in this task is the capacity to gather road parameters from the street framework itself, utilizing WSN just as crowd source information from street clients utilizing cell phones.

According to a research, as the number of cars increases, so does the measure of CO_2. The respondents in this study also noticed that constrained

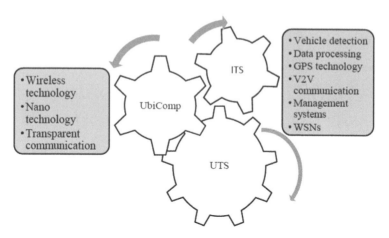

FIGURE 3.1
Ubiquitous transport systems.

mechanisms that furnish them with road conditions and featured those apparatuses may alleviate congestion.

Congestion is characterized as a situation where transport participants cannot move in an ideal or favorable manner. The intelligent traffic lights' performance was examined by simulations. It is seen that the future implementation will incorporate the ability to manage a system of junctions and ability to anticipate abnormal traffic streams described in Figure 3.2.

It alludes to the phenomenon wherein the capacity of infrastructure is surpassed. In any metropolitan city that is being utilized for the case study, the events of types of congestion are increasing; traffic jams happen largely during the mornings and afternoons as individuals travel regularly.

3.2 TRAFFIC CONGESTION MEASURING

Traffic congestion measurement falls in three groups:

- Basic measure
- Ratio measures
- Level of Service (LOS)

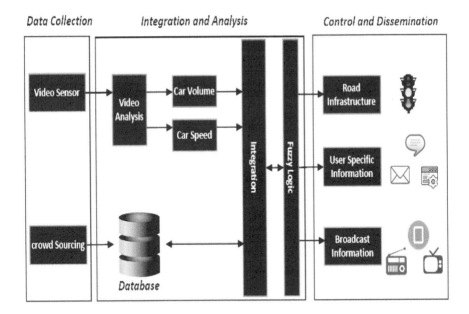

FIGURE 3.2
Architecture of smart traffic.

The congestion is proportional to increasing numbers of cars. The problem of these resources can be recovered by the use of IoT. Traffic lights cycle through the entry points in North, South, East, and West, giving each guide equivalent time toward let traffic through.

For example, there is one car on the N entry and eight cars on the S entry. The N entry will be given the same duration as S entry but the number of cars is lesser in N. The same scenario will be applicable for all scenarios of direction.

The second challenge is the unavailability of enough money to build new roads in some cases. The main factors that are used to monitor congestion are waiting time, rate of entering and leaving, and the number of queued cars. The impact of traffic is described in Figure 3.3.

The solution is to avail maximum road infrastructure when the number of cars increases. The challenges with this solution are that in most medium-sized cities, the land has been occupied by buildings and there's no place to build a new road.

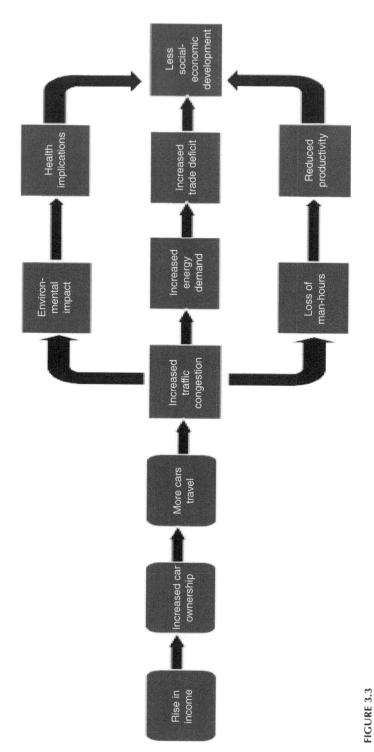

FIGURE 3.3
Impact of traffic.

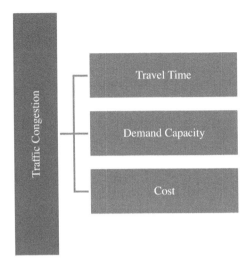

FIGURE 3.4
Traffic congestion.

3.3 TRAFFIC CONGESTION AND ITS CAUSES

There are various definitions of traffic congestion, each depending on the observer's perspective as shown in Figure 3.4.

If the vehicular volume on a transportation facility maximizes the potential of that facility, the output is a state of congestion. Whereas the number of road users is increasing, the availability of road networks is not increasing.

Non-recurring congestion can be called as unusual congestion that occurs by unforeseen environment.

The different types of congestion along with their descriptions are given in Table 3.1.

TABLE 3.1

Congestion Description

S.No.	Congestion Name	Description
1	Trigger-neck congestion	The narrowing of a lane causes the cars to generate a queue.
2	Bottlenecks	Several cars move from a network that has more lanes to one with fewer lanes.
3	Network control congestion	Off-peak traffic causes traffic jams.
4	Network morphology	Traffic jams on all adjacent sections

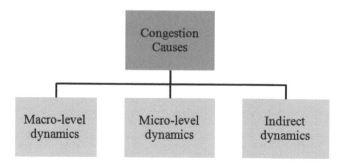

FIGURE 3.5
Causes of congestion.

3.3.1 Causes of Traffic Congestion

The causes of congestion are many cars on a road network, frequent modifications in the capacity of road infrastructure, driver performance, and society.

There are three clusters that are the main causes of congestion which are shown in Figure 3.5.

Macro-level dynamics
These are directly related to the status of the road.
Micro-level dynamics
These are associated with the demand of road facilities.
Indirect dynamics
There are no any specific constraints but it includes climatic conditions such as weather and events (Litman 2016).

Traffic congestion can be measured by LOS as it contains multiple parameters in it, as shown in Figure 3.6. The parameters to scale LOS are vehicle density, average vehicle speed, volume-to-capacity ratio, and delay.

Figure 3.7 shows the application of LOS in a multi-lane highway. The LOS with 'A' can be considered good and LOS with 'F' can be considered bad.

3.4 TRAFFIC MANAGEMENT USING COMPUTER VISION

Vehicle identification and tracking principles can be categorized by using UTS methodology. The methods of vehicle identification and tracking included the combined or separate application of spatial and temporal analysis on video sequences.

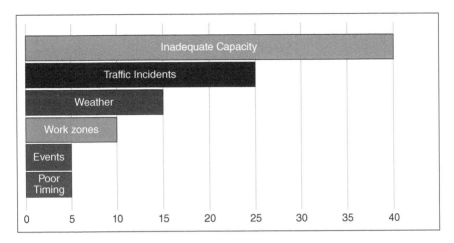

FIGURE 3.6
Parameters of LOS.

Level of Service	Flow Conditions	Operating Speed (mph)	Technical Descriptions
A		60	Highest level of service. Traffic flows freely with little or no restrictions on maneuverability. **No delays**
B		60	Traffic flows freely, but drivers have slightly less freedom to maneuver. **No delays**
C		60	Density becomes noticeable with ability to maneuver limited by other vehicles. **Minimal delays**
D		57	Speed and ability to maneuver is severely restricted by increasing density of vehicles. **Minimal delays**
E		55	Unstable traffic flow. Speeds vary greatly and are unpredictable. **Minimal delays**
F		<55	Traffic flow is unstable, with brief periods of movement followed by forced stops. **Significant delays**

FIGURE 3.7
Application of level of service.

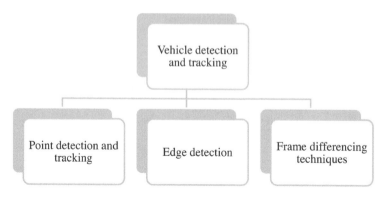

FIGURE 3.8
Ubiquitous transport systems.

Vehicle detection and tracking can be done by any of the methodologies given in Figure 3.8.

- Point Detection and Tracking

Irrespective of illumination, this approach is faster and gives consistent progress.

- Edge Detection

Morphological algorithms is implemented in the edge detection approach.

- Frame Differencing Techniques

The implementation is easier and gives great consistency with accurate results compared to the above methods such as point detection and tracking, edge detection; the only constraint is that the reference image is needed (Liphoto 2017).

3.5 WIRELESS SENSOR NETWORK'S ROLE IN SMART TRAFFIC

The trending technology of Wireless Sensor Network (WSN) is widely used in this modern world for a maximum range of applications for the best quality of human life. But due to their energy constrains, consumptions, and problems as mentioned above, these WSNs have their limitation in their application and their functionality. A typical WSN consists of various sensor components. These components combine to make a simple small device and this is implemented into various application scenarios. These advance specifications make them to be flexible when compared to the ordinary traditional networks. The applications of WSN are abundant; they are extremely scalable and have a high-density range due to their cheap rate and their smaller size.

Normally, all the sensor network protocols are designed with their own organizing capacity. Hence, these sensor network have an effective maintenance. They have forbearance against communication failure and the topology could change based on the nodes that could break down or be mobile or there can be depletion of energy.

Moreover, sensor nodes could be implemented in the rough environment to maintain the given task without any manpower. An embedded system played a major role in the past decade. These are very small in size, cheap, consume less power, and have many sensors which work in various environments.

Moreover, supplementary applications are inadequate due to some challenges associated with WSN. For instance, giving out capability is restricted and minimum rate of data in the nodes of the sensor couldn't warranty the maximum performance in some applications. When the communication range is very small, then there could be maximum energy consumption and network incompetence, since the requirement of multi-hop communications is often used for the transportation of data.

The high-drive restriction also directs to bad inspection, the development of data processing, as the energy gets drained rapidly and makes the network ineffective for the job. Low amount of energy consumed will maintain multi-hop communications work for a maximum duration. Despite its accuracy, energy constraint analysis from real exploitation can suffer many restrictions, since the data acquired by the sensors from a wide area are very tough to obtain. On the other hand, analytical/theoretical models obtained from the mathematical calculation offer huge exploration capacity, but they can be simplified through idealized hypotheses which could cause trouble during the practical implementation. WSN has become the most favored networking solution, although tremendously incomplete resources face serious threats. In addition, the nodes of sensors are very sensitive to some attacks which could be caused due to its lack of tamper-resistance. As a reliable technology and its architecture is presented in Figure 3.9, the WSN has been employed widely in other technologies such as IoT.

Numerous associated users have been exchanging data in WSNs. As one of the applications, the WSN is gaining reliability and popularity in network. WSN is considered as the most significant technology in the 21st century. WSN is considered as a vital component in linking the rational information world with the prevailing physical world despite the exposed working principle of WSN, information media, many threats to the security limit the claim of WSNs.

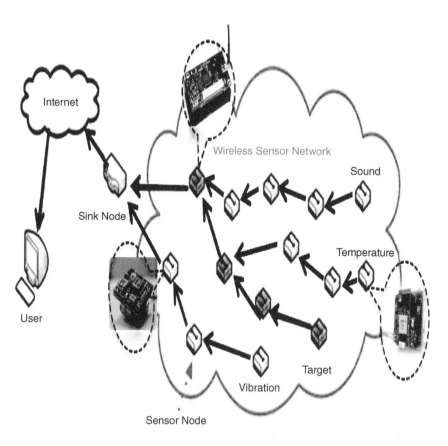

FIGURE 3.9
Architecture of WSN.

3.6 ENHANCE INTELLIGENT TRAFFIC LIGHT MANAGEMENT BY EMPLOYING PLC

A Programmable Logic Controller (PLC) plays a vital role in the field of microprocessor. It's very simple and easy for the users to handle since it could consist of hardware and software components, which could handle all the industrial components. The work of an engineer is to program the PLC using ladder logic, which could do certain type of automation and control in the industrial equipment. The greatest advantage of using PLC is that it can be reprogrammed depending on the user who handles it. It has an astounding effect on the automation since these PLC components are highly flexible and reliable at their implementation stage. Since the functionalities of the micro-controllers have been increased as well as their reduced cost had increased their scope and these lead to the use of micro controllers in several fields, PLC had been used in the field of hydraulics to control fluid flow in the place of electromechanical relays. In recent days, programmable logic controllers are established into a largely flexible component in the control system that can perform complicated mathematical calculations as well as work in a faster speed. Some leading PLC manufacturers are Allen Bradley, Honeywell, Siemens, Mitsubishi, Modicon, and so on.

In the Electro-Pneumatic system, the output is said to be the movement of solenoid. This could be done either by using relays or with the help of PLC. The work of the relay is to get the input signal from the various sensors and perform the function of normally opened or closed operation. With the movement, the solenoid is operated. This could also be done with the help of programmable logic controllers. The required logic diagram is made with the certain timers and sequential operation. At last, the signal is provided to the solenoid to the final control element to carry out the operation at various cylinders (Alam et al 2015).

There are four main features in control system engineering (Suresh et al 2020):

- Transfer of information
- Language-based variable usage
- Amendment of communication
- Utilization of multifaceted

3.6.1 Electro-Pneumatic Controllers

There are three main steps involved in the electro-pneumatic controllers:

1. Input devices could consist of various sensors and the signals obtained from them are transferred to the relays and controllers.
2. Signal processing devices consist of a set of relay switches or PLCs.
3. Output devices activate the solenoid to make a mechanical movement. These output devices can be an alarm or some indicators.

The electrical devices used in the controllers could be push buttons, limit switches, timers, relays, solenoids, temperature, and pressure switches. A sensor such as proximity sensors which is used in the indication of a certain thing and various electrical counters is also used. This controller combines the electrical and pneumatic technology which is largely used in much application. Either AC or DC source signal is applied here. Compressed air is used in this process as a medium of working. The operating voltage is around 12–220 V.

3.6.2 Programming a PLC

Programming a PLC is not a complicated task when a suitable programming technique is adopted. Many concepts can be used to enter a program in PLC:

1. Draw a ladder logic diagram,
2. Functional blocks,
3. Various Boolean expressions based on the low level, and
4. High-level programming language.

But the most commonly used method is the ladder logic diagram, which is an easy and efficient approach. This ladder logic could consist of programming logic in a way identical to the switching circuit. With the help of certain conventions, the ladder logic is converted into PLC ladder diagram. With the help of the cathode ray tube and the keyboard, it can integrate certain components into a logical ladder program. The input switches and relays are indicated in the form of a contact switches, olenoids, relays, counters, and timers are denoted as coils in the PLCs. Each step of a ladder program is denoted as rung. The program must place the necessary contacts and coils depending on the process. This could be verified rung by rung and the result could be displayed on a cathode-ray tube (CRT) screen.

The PLC ladder logic has two vertical lines which are also termed as rungs, which are supplied by a positive voltage from the left side and zero voltage from the right side. The horizontal lines (rungs) are in the middle of these vertical rungs which are the processes of the automation and the process could be carried out depending on the horizontal rung positions. Between these two sides are the horizontal rungs for the assumed power flow. Various operations are carried out in a PLC ladder diagram and they are arithmetic operations, timer operations, PLC bit logic operations, comparison operation, and timer operation (Alam et al 2015).

NO Contact of PLC: The representation of NO contact is to scan the input signal ON (1) in the specific bit address. When the signal is ON then the switch tends to close and performs the operation. It can be said that NO switch is opened normally; when the power flows, it will act as a closed switch.

NC Contact of PLC: This is exactly the opposite of the NO switch, which will scan the input signal OFF (0) in the specific bit address. When there is no signal then the switch tends to remain in the closed position, which gets opened when the signal is turned ON.

3.6.3 Push Button

A push button plays a major role in starting and stopping an operation. This could be indicated by an open-and-closed switch in a PLC diagram. There is also manually operated push button, which could be used for some emergency circumstances. The functionality of the push button is to move the position of the actuator into housing. This is supported by the spring mechanism which could open or close the contact. There are two types of push buttons, namely:

1. Momentary push button
2. Maintained contact push button

Momentary push buttons will come to their actual position once the button is manually released. The maintained push button which is mechanically latched has a certain latching mechanism to hold its position.

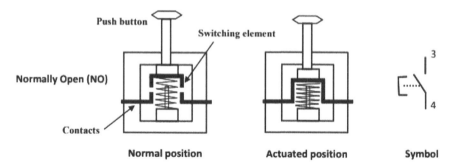

FIGURE 3.10
Operation of pushbutton when it is normally opened.

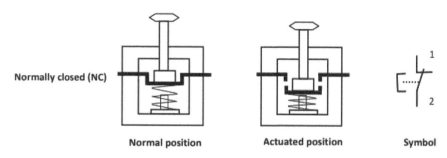

FIGURE 3.11
Operation of pushbutton when it is normally closed.

The pushbuttons can be categorized as Normally Opened (NO), Normally Closed (NC), and Change Over (CO) types.

At the position of NO, the switch is opened. During the actuator action, the contacts are closed which could permit the flow of air. At NC position, the air is forbidden. During the actuator position, the contacts are closed. Figures 3.10 and 3.11 represent the positions of the push buttons.

3.6.4 Limit Switches

Limit switches are like the push buttons. However, while the push buttons are manually operated, limit switches are said to be mechanically actuated. The switch, which could be a piston rod or a motor shaft, operates based on the position of the fluid. The limit switch provides an electric signal that provides an applicable system response.

The limit switch can be classified into two types, based on the actuation of the contacts (Li 2019).

1. Lever Actuated Contacts, in which the contacts operate at a very slow rate
2. Spring-loaded contacts that make the contacts to perform expeditiously

3.6.5 Pressure Switches

Pneumatic-electric signal conversion is done with the help of the pressure switch. The work of the pressure switch is to detect the transformation of pressure change. With this information, the electrical switch will be opened and closed when a prearranged pressure point is attained. Diaphragm or bellows will act as a pressure sensor. The change in the pressure is detected by the diaphragm which is in the form a plate that contracts and expands. In this similar way, the bellows also react to pressure change. The pressure that comes through the inlet is noticed. When this pressure reaches a limit, then the diaphragm or the bellows will expand which will make a spring-loaded plunger to break/make the contact.

3.6.6 Solenoids

In the electro-pneumatic controllers, the control valve which is electrically operated to actuate is the part which forms as an interaction layer. The important activity of the directional control valves is to regulate the supply of air (i.e., it should either switch to ON or OFF position), compression, and rarefaction of the cylinder drives. This switching operation could be made possible with the help of the solenoid.

The mode of operation is of two types:

1. Spring valves which return to their position until the power supply is provided to the solenoid.
2. Double solenoid valves cling to the finally operated state although the solenoid is not supplied with the voltage.

During the first step, every solenoid will not be energized and hence the directional control valve does not operate, which makes it inactive. There is no beginning position for the double valve since it will not return the spring to its position.

The numerous ways in which the solenoid operates are of the following:

1. 3/2 Way single solenoid valve, spring return
2. 5/2 Way single solenoid valve, spring return
3. 5/2 Way single double solenoid valve

3.6.7 Relays

This is a very simple device which could withstand any harsh environment and these relays are said to be electromagnetically operated. These relay switches act as signal-processing devices. The relays are designed in such a manner as to withstand the heavy power surges which could cause damage to the circuits. The system consists of the coil core through which the voltage is applied. This coil converts the electrical power into the electromagnetic energy which will attract the armature toward the winding. The armature will actuate the relay, making it to be in the open or closed position. Depending upon this operation, the system provides the output. There is a spring attached in order to return the armature to the initial position. There is an interlocking capacity supported by the relays. This interlocking capacity will avoid the instantaneous switching of relays to ON and OFF. The relays are indicated by K1, K2, and K3. The relay contact with its operation is indicated in the Figure 3.12.

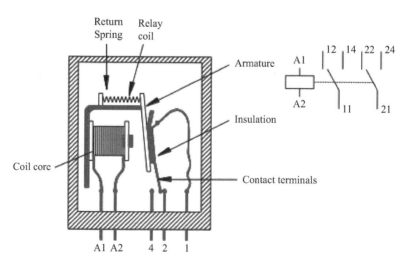

FIGURE 3.12
Cross-sectional view of relay.

3.6.8 Timers for Traffic Lights

Timers play a major role in the PLC. In the pneumatic process, when one side of the cylinder expands then the other side should contract, and this process is done successfully with the help of timers which could provide certain delay in the times of expansion and compression. Every control task which is automated needs a time to perform perfectly.

These time delays find their own memory spaces in the system. The representation of the timer circuit purely depends on the manufacturer. The timer implemented in the PLCs is in the form of the software module and it could provide the digital way of representing the timing. The typical PLCs could have timers with the bit address of 64, 128, 256, 512, and many more.

The timers in the ladder program could be indicated as T1 and T2. To explicitly reset timer, the logic of 1 should be applied to the reset port.

The timers are of two types, namely:

- On delay timer
- Off delay timer

On Delay Timer

When the signal is received in the start input signal, the timer will be in the ON state. The output signal changes from 1 to 0, till the preset timing is attained (there will be a delay in the timing operation). When the signal reaches a preset timing, then the output will be changed from 0 to 1. The function of on-delay timer is described in Figure 3.13.

Off-Delay Timer

This is exactly the opposite of the on-delay timer. When the start input is provided with some signal, then the timer starts to operate and gives the

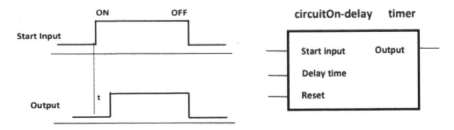

FIGURE 3.13
Circuit diagram of on-delay timers with their timing variations.

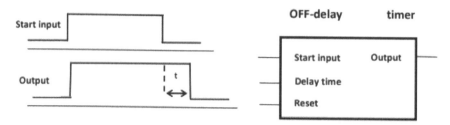

FIGURE 3.14
Circuit diagram of off-delay timers with their timing variations.

output 1. When the result logic changes from 1 to 0, then the timer will not stop at a sudden. There is a delay in their off time till a preset time. When this time is reached, the output will change to 0. The function of off-delay timer is described in Figure 3.14.

3.6.9 Counters

The count of the events and the particles kept to the process is indicated with the help of the counters. The controllers should be operated with the help of the counters. For instance, let's see the bottle-filling mechanism. The counter counts the number of bottles which is to be filled with the solution. When the conveyor belt moves, the counter counts the bottles kept in the conveyor belt. This could be used in the place of a sorting device.

There are two types of counters:

1. Up counter: In this counter, the accumulator value will be increased to 1 till the input sets to true.
2. Down counter: This works by decrementing the accumulator value until a preset value is reached. The circuit diagram of up and down counter is shown in Figure 3.15.

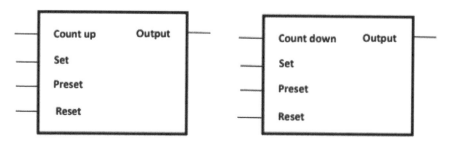

FIGURE 3.15
Circuit diagram of up and down counter.

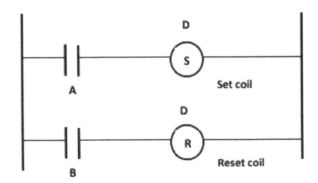

FIGURE 3.16
Ladder logic diagram to indicate the latching function.

3.6.10 Memory Elements

The transitional values are placed in the memory elements. They are represented as flags. The operation is performed by set and reset coil in the ladder diagram. The diagram below shows the set and the reset coil. Let us denote the output as D. When the switch A gets closed, then the latch sets itself to logic 1 and the output will be 1. This output remains until the switch B performs its operation. When the switch is opened then also latching operation is continued. When the switch B gets opened, then unlatching process takes place which will set the output D as 0. Figure 3.16 describes the ladder logic diagram to indicate the latching function.

3.6.11 Replacement of Equipment with the Ladder Diagram

Relays are said to be electro-magnetic switches. Here, it is explained with the help of a small example of wiring a relay circuit into a ladder diagram. This is very necessary since the PLC does not understand code. Many PLCs convert the ladder diagram into coding.

The following are the steps to be carried out.

Step 1: The PLC doesn't care about the external equipment and devices. These devices should be indicated by a ladder symbol. For instance, the input devices are not cared by the PLC. Either it analyzes whether the given input is ON or OFF and the process it does is considered.

Step 2: The input voltage is very necessary. The AC supply is not considered. Rather, the voltage for the process to get in operation is considered which is indicated in the form of two vertical bars (rungs) for the positive voltage and the ground.

Step 3: This could be indicated in the form of a circular symbol. This could be a bell, an alarm, or a motor.

Step 4: It must be indicated whether the PLC is loaded (which means addressing a device). Then, the process is done rung by rung in a horizontal manner. These could be seen in the Modicon equipment. The program does its operation and it can set the switch to automatic or manually operated, depending on the user who handles the equipment.

Step 5: Other than this, it has a temperature switch which could sense the temperature. These switches can be wired either normally opened or normally closed, depending on the temperature variations. Other than these, a sensor plays a major role in the field of PLC.

3.6.12 Schematic Diagram

The schematic diagram of PLC wiring with the ladder logic of a pneumatic controller is shown in Figure 3.17.

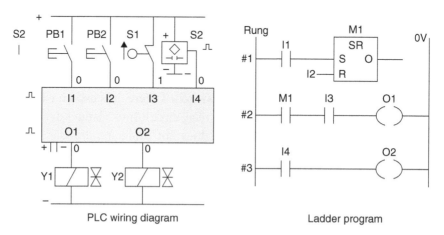

PLC wiring diagram   Ladder program

FIGURE 3.17
PLC wiring with the ladder logic of a pneumatic controller.

3.7 CONCLUSION

The pneumatic controller with the implementation of the PLC is quite easy since it reduces the size, is easy to maintain, consumes very less voltage, has less cost and is highly accurate, and is easily programmable. Although, it has some difficulties in finding the error and wiring becomes a challenging task, especially for certain temperatures and vibrations. In traffic lights, two strategies such as fixed and real-time are used. The static works with preset timing, the signal period shown on the light is pre-set from experience, giving no consideration to the current status.

4

An Intelligent Airport System Using Artificial Intelligence (AI) Algorithm

4.1 INTRODUCTION TO INTELLIGENT AIRPORT

As nation's critical infrastructure, the Indian Department of Homeland Security describes the critical services that establish nation's society and serve as the backbone of its economy, security, and health.

The Airport Organizational Boundary depicts what is controlled or owned by the airport authority or management, and deals with the design and configuration of airport infrastructure and the operational processes and procedures for the enough efficiency of its own organization. Figure 4.1 shows the groups of this boundary (Chen et al 2015).

There are many challenges encountered in implementing secured smart airport and a flight has to deal with them and adapt its systems so as to overcome challenges which include a reliable airport surveillance radar. However, adaptation is not an easy task because of not only the complex and sensitive operations but also the costly components of airports.

Airport Service Boundary, as shown in Figure 4.2, integrates the airport supply and support services such as surveillance and lies outside the direct management control of the airport authority.

4.1.1 Artificial Intelligence

It can be called as machine intelligence, where airports are performing the cognitive functions of human beings to reduce the work of manpower explained in Figure 4.3.

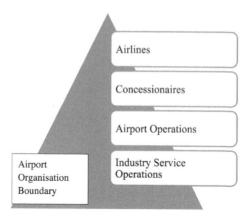

FIGURE 4.1
Airport organization.

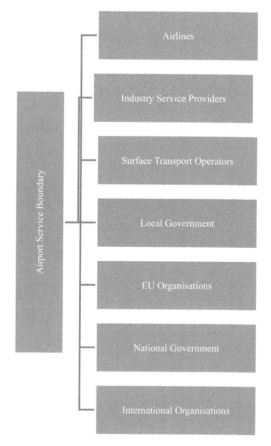

FIGURE 4.2
Airport surveillance and service.

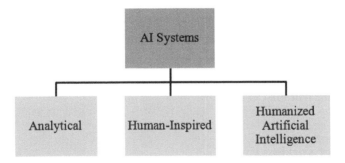

FIGURE 4.3
Artificial intelligence systems.

4.2 CHARACTERISTIC OF SMART AIRPORT

According to the Airport Cooperative Research Program (ACRP), the IT system architecture of airports can be organized in four conceptual categories of layers explained in Figure 4.4.

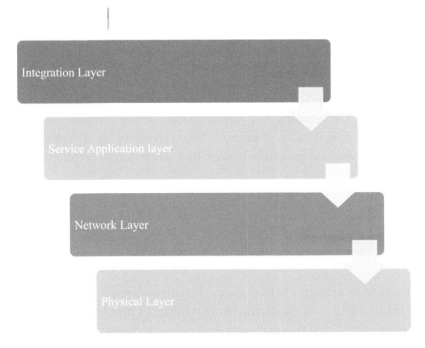

FIGURE 4.4
Layers of airport.

4.2.1 Physical Layer

- This layer consists of the cabling and fiber infrastructure that is considered as foundation for computer systems which are in use at the airport. Furthermore, it includes non-electronic physical components (Jeeradist et al 2016).

4.2.2 Networking Layer

These systems underpinning the network layer to communicate data and information with the use of the wired or wireless infrastructure (Lee and Park 2016). Routers, switches, gateways, and wireless access points are the physical components (Padrón et al 2016).

4.2.3 Service Application Layer

It encompasses all the systems for the working of airports. By using the service application layer, it contains a set of standards and methods to produce design with the support of service-oriented computing environment.

4.2.4 Integration Layer

It gives entire applications that are needed to operate the airports for organizing and sharing the information among themselves (Pigni et al 2016). Specifically, it permits the systems to be directly linked together as well as share information in order to make better-informed decisions.

4.3 CHALLENGES FOR SMART AIRPORT

The idea of smart airports faces many challenges. Some of these challenges are the resource constraints, the rising volumes of travelers that should be accommodated, and the increasing demands of tech-savvy passengers and tenants. Here, every aspect of airport operation can have challenges, from

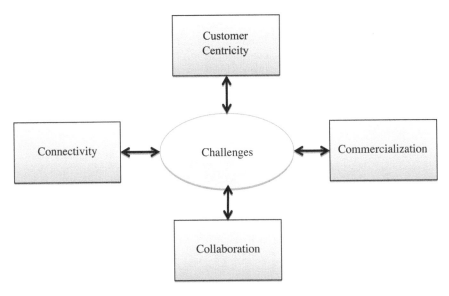

FIGURE 4.5
Challenges encountered in a smart airport.

passenger management and communications to commercial activities and aircraft turnarounds, which are explained in Figure 4.5.

Customer centrality makes the passenger's experience easier and more convenient at every step (Straker and Cara 2016). In the last few years, airports and airlines give a high priority to the improvement of customer service as they are the stakeholders. Intelligent airports have the vision for travelers to be able to drop off bags on arrival and departure.

4.3.1 Characteristics of Airport

Connectivity is responsible for today's optimum passenger experience. It has ubiquitous connectivity for other Cs (Customer, Collaboration, and Commercialization) to succeed. Specifically, passengers always connect their smartphones and mobile devices to all relevant airport systems. On the other hand, at the intelligent airports, no one is stationary (Yang et al 2006). Characteristics of an airport are described in Figure 4.6.

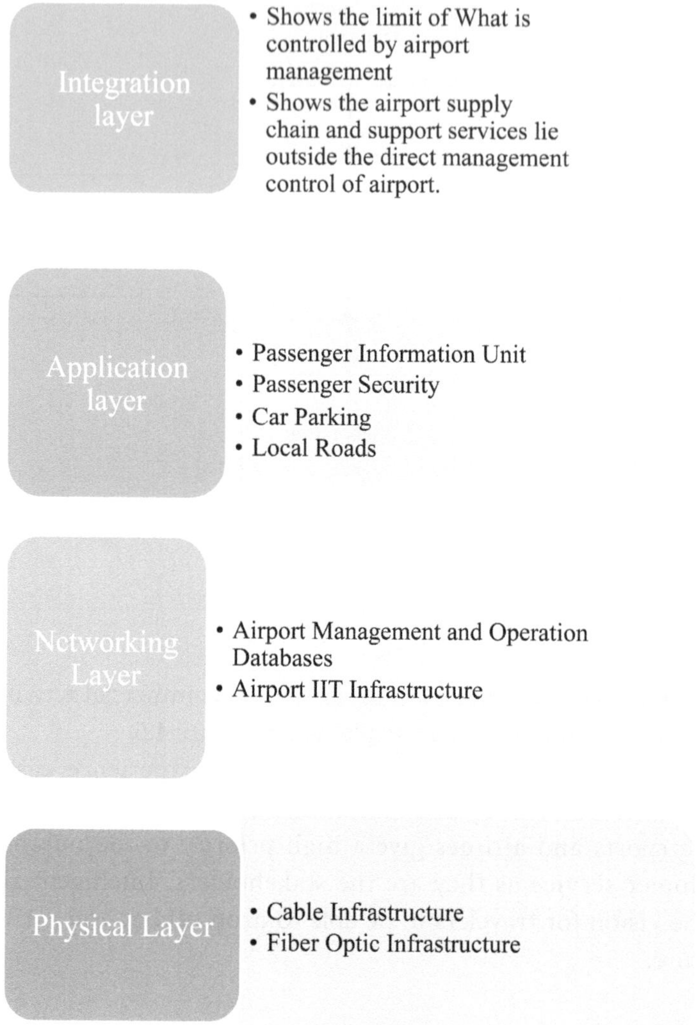

Integration layer
- Shows the limit of What is controlled by airport management
- Shows the airport supply chain and support services lie outside the direct management control of airport.

Application layer
- Passenger Information Unit
- Passenger Security
- Car Parking
- Local Roads

Networking Layer
- Airport Management and Operation Databases
- Airport IIT Infrastructure

Physical Layer
- Cable Infrastructure
- Fiber Optic Infrastructure

FIGURE 4.6
Characteristics of an airport.

Commercialization is another challenge that smart airports facing nowadays. Commercialization maximizes the existing revenue streams and creates new ones. According to passenger analytic, it is easy to understand the way passengers move through the airport.

4.4 SMART ASSETS AND ASSET GROUPS OF THE AIRPORT

More specifically, based on ISO 27005, primary assets are those core information and processes which support the important airport activities, including business.

Here, secondary assets are those assets where primary elements depend, and they are vulnerable to cyber security threats because the attackers want to weaken the primary assets, comprising processes and information processes and activities.

Figure 4.7 represents the smart assets such as airline operation, airport administration, IT, customer ancillary services, facilities, and maintenance. Tables 4.1, 4.2, and 4.3 show smart assets and group enabling smart airports, smart assets in terms facilities and IT groups, and smart asset group in passenger management, safety and security, respectively.

Airport surveillance radars are used for detecting and tracking planes in the terminal airspace surrounding an airport. The terminal airspace

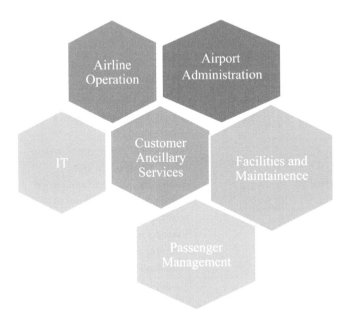

FIGURE 4.7
Smart asset.

TABLE 4.1

Smart Assets and Group Enabling Smart Airports

Smart Asset Group	Smart Asset
Airline/Airside operations	Air traffic management (ATM), Navigation aid and approach
	De-icing method
	Airfield lighting, Railway control monitoring systems
	Flight tracking
	Cargo processing systems
	Airport operation database (AODB)
	Departure control system
	Airport resource and infrastructure management system
Administration of airport	Human resource management system
	Enterprise management system
	Procurement management system
	Financial management system
	Policy management system
Customer ancillary services	Mobile payment
	Point of sales machines

TABLE 4.2

Smart Assets in Facilities and IT Groups

Smart Asset Group	Smart Asset
Facilities and maintenance	Control building system
	Computerized management system
	Elevators and lifts
	Environment management system
	Energy management system
External IT	Cloud-based data and application
	Global positioning system
	Network security management
	Passenger airline communication system
	Wide area network
External IT	Flight display system and management
	IT equipment
	Virtual private network
	Stored data
	Wi-Fi
	Log monitoring and event notification

TABLE 4.3

Smart Assets in Passenger Management and Safety and Security

Smart Asset Group	Smart Asset
External IT	Fuel management
	Lightning detection system
	Electronic parking toll
	Transport (public & private)
	Vehicle identification
Passenger management	Central reservation system
	Logistics system within airport
	Passenger name records
	Passenger check in and boarding
	Stationary devices
Safety and security	Access control system
	Authentication system
	Screening of passengers
	Immigration
	Emergency systems
	Perimeter intrusion detection system

consists of 50–60 NM radius centered on the airport. Tracking aircraft can be done by fan-shaped beams, Pulse Repetition Frequency (PRF), rapid antenna scan rates, and Radio Frequency (RF) diversity.

4.5 SMART RADAR FOR AIRPORT SURVEILLANCE

Airport Surveillance Radar (ASR) is air traffic control system which is used to detect the presence and the location of aircraft at the airport. It controls the traffic for around 96 km with the atmospheric feet of 25,000. There are five major parts in RADAR are:

- Waveguides
- Antenna
- Duplexer
- Receiver
- Threshold Decision

The radar types and applications are shown in Figure 4.8
  Types of RADAR

- Pulsed RADAR
- Continuous RADAR

RADAR Applications

- Military
- Air Traffic Control
- Space
- Ground Traffic Control

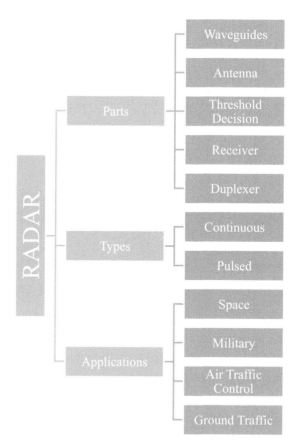

FIGURE 4.8
RADAR types and their applications.

Active Electronically Scanned Array (AESA) radar is widely used in many fields where it serves majorly in military. In this approach, Support Vector Machines (SVM) are used. SVM is a classification algorithm. Here, for the detection of the track, we could use various sensors that could follow the principle of micro-Doppler's effect. Then, the track detected should be classified based on the high-end machine learning algorithm. Here, classification could be done based on the statistics. Then, these statistical data should be compared. Comparison and the classification could be either discriminative or generative. The adequacy of SVM could be used for this purpose.

By introducing intelligence to airports, an improved planning of their budget and resources will be supplied that will allow more effectual management of passengers' demands. In order to make it easily accessible to everyone, the requirement of smarter airport arises that makes a digital connection among the system and process.

According to European Union Agency for Cyber security (ENISA), smart airports run on a network that is capable to produce responses with the data obtained, on the one hand, supply passengers with an improved and flawless journey and, on the other hand, provide high security level for the passengers as well as the operators. The travelers' experience could also be improved by promoting a quality service with the high-tech components. Alternatively, the smart airport can provide highly reliable service that enhances the sustainability by undergoing the area that is related to the efficiency, safety, growth, and protection. To achieve these facilities, the airport should have enough aircraft with the genuine number of passengers and optimum fee structure. The non-aeronautical revenue could also be increased; that includes parking, food, advertising, and so on.

Services can be added that provide high passenger satisfaction by promoting enhanced service at the airport. The province of efficiency can be defined as the development of equipped efficiency with the augmented integration and the next level of stakeholder association. These outcomes reduce the cost thereby developing the available assets with the well-equipped infrastructure arrangement and availability. This could also increase the social responsibility that makes the airport environmentally friendly with the "green" solutions. The security threats should be handled in a well-equipped manner thereby enhancing the safety and decreasing the disturbances in operations.

4.5.1 End-to-End Passenger Journey

Factors such as volatile fuel prices and the worldwide financial crisis created the need of reshaping the aviation industry with new strategies in order to survive the economic realities. Even though airports are still profitable, they may face a decline in passengers, whether they travel for business or for leisure. Accordingly, this will impact revenue.

The solution to the decreasing number of passengers is to deliver a more pleasant passenger experience. It can be accomplished only if airport management deeply understands the passengers, in terms of demographics, behaviors, attitudes, and needs. In order to deliver a pleasant experience, a strong collaboration among airlines and airports is needed. This collaboration depends on airlines and airports sharing passengers' data because this will help the management to understand the real needs that passenger have and design services and products that will attract passengers.

On the other hand, income that comes from parking and food-and-beverage providers has contributed a great deal to an airport's revenue mix for decades. For this reason, such sources are important components of the airports' total revenue.

Airports should focus on areas such as retail, hospitality, parking, and real-estate, and design new services. In order to achieve a pretty high value for each service, it is advisable to adopt a customer-centric approach, to gain a better passenger experience. On the other hand, the increased number of security measures, dealing with long lines, missed connections, and changed gates are frequent problems that should be solved.

The above problems drive to the development of an end-to-end passenger experience framework that offers some advantages for both airports and airlines. First, this approach offers a high chance to up-sell and cross-sell services based on genuine data and status of the travel environment. For instance, airports can offer valet parking to travelers arriving late for a flight, or hospitality services in the event of a delay.

Both the AESA and PESA (Passive Electronically Scanned Array) radar consist of numerous antennas and transmitters. The main variation between the AESA and PESA radar is that the former could generate its own microwave signal with its altering phase, i.e., it is able to change its angle position (from one azimuth angle to another). They can be operated at varied frequencies (around 1000 frequency in a second). The major problem that arises here is occurrence of false alarm due to the sensor indication. This could be caused due to the certain unwanted object that could fall on the track giving a disturbance to the object of interest. Certain measures could be taken to control it. It is known that machine learning algorithm has raised its head into every invention and technologies since it could make a machine to learn by its own.

4.6 SUPPORT VECTOR MACHINES APPROACH FOR CLASSIFICATION

SVMs are one of the supervised learning models in machine learning that are employed for analysis or classification or regression. In an SVM model, the training/test samples are represented as dot/points in the space and they are mapped in such a way that the clear gap among the categories appears which separates the samples. New test samples/examples are later mapped on the Using the Kernel trick, where SVMs are also be able to perform non-linear classification in addition to linear classification. SVMs automatically map the inputs with high dimensional feature/attribute spaces.

SVM hyperplane is the only responsible for good separation of training data with the largest distance to its nearby data. This approach is generally known as functional margin. The state of the rule is, if margin is larger than the generalization error of classifier will be lower.

If the detected tracks of n points is given and the method of it is $(-x \to 1, y1)$ .... $(-x \to n, yn)$ and here yi is 1, this indicates the class with the sample $\to -xi$ is present. Each $\to -xi$ is a real vector of p-dimension. Our interest is detecting the "extreme- margin hyper plane," which separates the category of samples from $\to -xi$. This is required to be definite to maximize the distance among the hyper plane as well as the adjacent sample $\to -xi$.

It is understandable that H1 usually does not disconnect the classes. While H2 separates them by a minute margin, on the other hand, H3 disconnects them with the greatest margin. The hyperplane is defined as the set of points $\to -x$ satisfying $\to -x * \to -w - b = 0$. The support vector contains the sample on the margin. The offset of the hyperplane from the origin with normal vector $\to -w$ *is* determined by the parameter $\to -w$.

Hard-margin two parallel hyperplanes, which separate two classes of data, can be selected if the training data are linearly separable. So, by this it can have the distance between them is as possible as large (Elish and Elish 2008). The "margin" is nothing but the region bounded by these two hyperplanes. The maximum margin hyperplane lies between these planes. These hyperplanes can be described by the equations

$$\to -w \text{ }^* \to -x - b = 1$$

and

$$\to -w \text{ }^* \to -x - b = -1$$

$\to -w$ is the distance between two hyperplanes,

Hereby, minimizing w can maximize the distance between the planes. By adding the constraint: for each either $\to -w \text{ }^* \to -x - b \geq 1$ or $\to -w \text{ }^* \to -x - b \leq 1$ if $yi = -1$, here the data points can be prevented from falling into the margin.

According to the constraints/conditions, every point of the data should be on the definite plane of the margin. Equation 4.1 is the modified equation:

$$yi(\vec{w} \text{ }^* \vec{x} - b) \geq 1, \text{ } for \text{ } all \text{ } 1 \leq I \leq n \tag{4.1}$$

To get the optimization problem, it can be combined.

Decrease $\vec{w}$ subject to $\vec{w} \text{ }^* \vec{x} - b \geq 1$ for $I = 1,2,3,.n.$ completely. The max-margin hyperplane is determined by over right arrow (xi), which lies at the near end. Here, the $\vec{x}$ is named as *support vectors*.

Soft margin is the loss function with the equation max $(0,1 - yi(\vec{w} \text{ }^* \vec{x} - b))$. It is introduced to enhance SVM where the data are non-linearly separable.

If the constraint in Equation. 4.1 is satisfied then this function value is zero, which means,

$\to -x$ is in the right margin side.

The function with minimization is given in Equation 4.2.

$$High(0,1 - yi(\vec{w} \text{ }^* \vec{x} - b)) + \lambda \vec{w} \tag{4.2}$$

Here, λ increments the values of margin-size and making sure that the $\vec{x}$ is fall/separated with the actual side of it. Therefore, the soft margin SVM may behave like hard margin SVM for enough small values of λ in the case when linearly classifiable test data are available.

4.7 EVALUATION

Here, employing feature vector in order to detect the tracks. The tracks are detected by the radar range equation (Equation 4.3).

$$R = (G_t G_r P_1 \lambda^2 \sigma \mid (4\pi)^3 KT_0 BF(SNR)_{min} L)^{(1/4)} \qquad (4.3)$$

Where,

G_t, G_r – Transceiver gain
P_1 – Power transmitted
Σ – Radar cross-section
$(SNR)_{min}$ – Minimum signal-to-noise ratio
L – System loss factor

With the help of the radar Range equation, it is possible to obtain the raw data. The classification procedure starts with the raw data. This stage involves the filtering stage. Then, the data are fed into the detection algorithm.

At this stage, the features are extracted from the data. Then, the extracted targets are forwarded to classification. The various processed data are quantified before the classification. This utilizes the statistical methods and sends to the training phase after favoritism. The procedure repeats for the occurred target which is shown in the flow chart given in Figure 4.9.

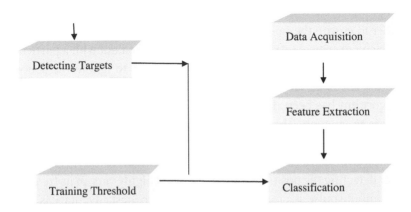

FIGURE 4.9
Flow chart representing the track estimation with machine learning process.

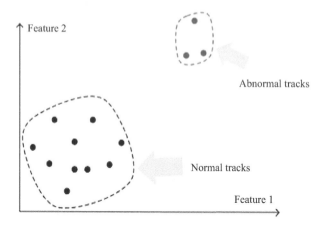

FIGURE 4.10
Detection of abnormal tracks using SVM.

The intrusion detection algorithm could be employed at this stage. The similar detected tracks that are trained with the predefined characteristic set come under one type where the remaining track with certain disturbances comes on the other side which is shown in Figure 4.10.

4.8 CONCLUSION

The technological evolutions make daily routine to be updated and upgraded in all aspects of life. The introduction of IoT in industrial environments is not as simple as it is shown. A new cycle of tests and measurements should be held in order to ensure the safety and security. Specifically, the adoption of such technology to critical infrastructures must be carried out with a particularly careful handling. Through this chapter, a solution to ignore the abnormal track and the necessary track action taken using high-end machine learning algorithm has been discussed. The impacts of AESA radar technology are large in aviation. These technologies are highly adapted in the field of air and naval forces that use AESA radar to detect minute targets at a wider range. Electronic surveillance system finds it difficult to vary in its frequencies for detecting the position. But, AESA could highly vary in its frequencies with a minute pulse at a random sequence. The greatest advantage is to resist jammers. But a minor disadvantage is that since it could show variations in its frequencies, this system could no longer persist in its lifetime.

5

An Effective IoT Framework for the Healthcare Environment

5.1 A BRIEF INTRODUCTION TO HEALTHCARE ENVIRONMENT

Healthcare is a medical care for monitoring the patients whether they are normal or abnormal, and using preventive methods to ensure their health.

The technology used in healthcare is in two aspects which are:

1. Computing tools for healthcare
2. Enabling it 24/7

Most of the healthcare technologies enhance current health delivery model but pervasive healthcare follows a **"from doctor-based to patient-centric,"** healthcare delivery model (Chan, 2015; Peng et al 2020). The sample healthcare architecture is given in Figure 5.1.

Medical technologies are always most important as managing health and quality of life is an urgent task (Vermesan et al 2015). IoT has access to health monitoring, and results in the quality improvement and cost deduction. With the application of smart things support, patients and the physician diagnose the disease efficiently (Zhang et al 2018). The improvement potential of different systems is shown in Figure 5.2.

The current methods with external sensors and mobile phones are outdated. Healthcare systems may be least efficient in some cases, when comparing with other systems and these can be improved in many ways. As of now, 20% of medical errors are due to diagnostic errors, not only by incorrect diagnosis method but also due to the delay of treatment. Connected healthcare devices have strength to increase

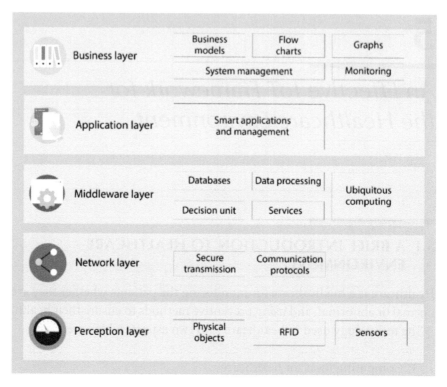

FIGURE 5.1
Healthcare architecture (Sklyar and Sokolova 2019).

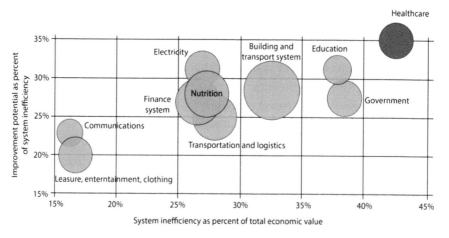

FIGURE 5.2
Improvement potential of different systems.

Instrumented
Measure and sense the current condition permanently

- Smart health solutions automatically capture information to proactively manage conditions and deliver preventive, therapeutic care
- Sensors that recognize physical changes such as pressure, motion, blood status, or temperature are embedded in wearable devices or other equipment

Interconnected
Devices in system communicate, share data with each other

- Smart health systems remove information barriers and seamlessly integrate data and analytics into healthcare processes to enable better decisions and comprehensive, coordinated healthcare
- Mobile and home-based devices monitor vital signs and activities in real time and communicate with personal health record services, PCs and smartphones, caregivers and healthcare professionals

Intelligent
Able to predict and to respond on unplaned events

- Smarter health systems continually analyze information from multiple devices and other sources to derive insights and recommendations for the individual's health regimes
- Analytics programs monitor device data and use rules and logic to compare against targets, track progress against goals, and send alerts when needed

FIGURE 5.3
Characteristics of smart healthcare solution.

the patient monitoring and decision-making by a doctor, by collecting and analyzing patient data and medical resources (Vermesan et al 2015). Figure 5.3 shows the various characteristics of smart healthcare solution.

Many health devices have connectivity issues; however, there are some innovative products in the market, which are already showing the tendency of IoT in healthcare (Islam et al 2015). Figure 5.4 depicts the components of healthcare IoT.

5.2 RELATED WORK

The development of healthcare system could increase the healthcare of anyone at anytime and anywhere, thereby decreasing the time and other constraints with the increase in coverage and the quality (Pramanik et al 2017).

Remote consultation, commonly known as teleconsultation, has gained a lot of importance these days (Islam et al 2015). This procedure uses a bidirectional control technology with high-resolution images in a bandwidth network (Jayalakshmi and Gomathi 2018).

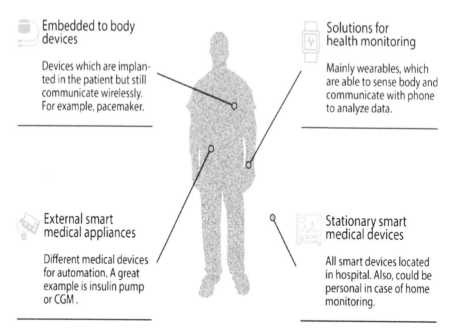

Embedded to body devices

Devices which are implanted in the patient but still communicate wirelessly. For example, pacemaker.

Solutions for health monitoring

Mainly wearables, which are able to sense body and communicate with phone to analyze data.

External smart medical appliances

Different medical devices for automation. A great example is insulin pump or CGM.

Stationary smart medical devices

All smart devices located in hospital. Also, could be personal in case of home monitoring.

FIGURE 5.4
Components of healthcare IoT.

5.3 ANN FOR REAL-TIME MONITORING

The fundamental part in neural network is termed as perceptron. A perceptron contains several inputs, a processor, and a single output. A perceptron pursues the model known as the "feed-forward model," which means that the inputs are received through a neuron and are thus processed; the result is produced as output. There are four main processes in perceptron which are listed below:

1. Receive inputs,
2. Weigh inputs,
3. Sum inputs
4. Generate outputs.

Each and every input which is received by a neuron must be slanted, i.e., multiplied by some value. Generating a perceptron usually starts by conveying random weights. Every input is taken individually and multiplied by its weight. The generation of the output takes place by transferring the sum throughout an activation function.

If it is a simple binary output, then activation function tells whether the perceptron is to be "fired" or not. For instance,

- If the sum is positive number, then 1 will be the output.
- If the sum is negative, then –1 will be the output.

Additional factor to be considered is bias. If both the inputs are equal to zero, then any sum would be zero which is independent of multiplicative weight.

To end this problem, a third input is summed which is called as the bias input with a value of 1.

The steps involved in training the perceptron are:

1. Afford the perceptron with inputs of well-known response.
2. Inquire the perceptron to deduce a response.
3. Calculate the error.
4. Regulate all the weights, and then repeat from step 1.

This process is repeated until the results obtained are satisfactory. Then, it must link all the perceptrons in layers in the input and in the output, in order to produce a neural network. The layers amid the input and the output will be a hidden layer.

5.3.1 Machine Learning Algorithms

There are five methods in the classification technique based on various mathematical concepts. These divisions are based on

1. Statistics
2. Distance
3. Decision Tree
4. Neural Network
5. The Rule

5.3.2 K-Nearest Neighbor

In K-NN, the nearer neighbors used more than far objects for computing the weight in both cases of classification and regression.

- d is the distance to the neighbor with weight 1/d.
- k is the constant given by the user.

In k-NN, no training step is required and hence it is receptive to the confined distribution of data.

Training example has a class label and it is represented in the vector form of the feature space in multi-dimensions The test point in the classification part is assigned the label that is nearest in the training of k samples. Euclidean distance is used for continuous variables, whereas hand hamming distance is used for text classification of discrete variables.

The performance of K-NN can also be improved by learning the distance matrix and analysis of neighborhood components. The point to be renowned here is every three distance measures are merely legitimate for the continuous variables. The hamming distance must be used in the case of categorical variables.

5.4 DECISION TREE ALGORITHM

It possesses decisions set which will produce the dataset classification rules. Every leaf node is allocated to a record that begins from the root and then traversing to a child node.

Decision tree can be constructed in two ways:

1. Build a tree
2. Prune it

5.5 CHALLENGES IN FEATURE SELECTION

While determining an attribute subset, it is very hard to measure its cost. Selecting the subset of attributes with minimal risk and low cost is a thread which is significant in defining its class or pattern.

Usually, attributes are classified into three types:

1. Relevant: Output depends on attributes
2. Irrelevant: Output does not depend on attributes
3. Redundant: Role of an attribute is interchanged

The purpose of attribute assortment is to determine the finest subset containing "m" attributes as of "n" attributes. During attribute selection, an exhaustive search strategy must be applied in order to explore the best subset among all possible attribute subsets, which may result in a substantially immense computational complexity.

Using an alternative approach for optimal selection in computational complexity may result in many possible solutions but fails to assure in the event of detecting whether the finally selected attribute is globally optimal or not.

An attribute congruity falls in two ways (Suresh et al 2020):

1. Univariate approach
2. Multivariate approach

5.5.1 Univariate Approach

Univariate strategies are flexible in terms of speed and structure.

5.5.2 Multivariate Approach

Initially, it can be used in almost every environment, majorly in settings. Additionally, when managing a large attribute arena, it becomes expensive (Suresh et al 2020).

5.6 SUPPORT VECTOR MACHINES (SVM)

SVMs are one of the supervised learning models in machine learning, employed for an analysis. These are binary, linear, and non-probabilistic classifiers. In SVM model, the training/test samples are represented as dot/points in the space and they are mapped in such a way that a clear gap among the categories appears which separates the samples.

New test samples/examples are later mapped on the kernel trick. SVMs are also able to perform non-linear classification in addition to linear classification.

SVM hyperplane is responsible for the separation of training data with the largest distance to its nearby data. This approach is generally known as functional margin. The state of the rule is if margin is larger, the generalization error of classifier will be lower. This shapes to voracious search for a tolerable decision tree.

TABLE 5.1

Wireless Sensor Network Description

S. No.	Wireless Sensor	Description
1	Microcontroller	Has computational abilities of the platform
2	Radio transceiver	Has low-power wireless communications
3	Sensor board	Has hardware interfaces to external sensors
4	Power Layer	Has power through batteries, capacitors

5.7 AN EFFECTIVE IoT FRAMEWORK FOR INTELLIGENT HEALTHCARE MONITORING

Here, the proposed methodology employs healthcare approach, and the system implements certain procedures like data sensing and processing of information. The components of wireless sensor network (WSN) along with its description are given in Table 5.1.

The MICROCHIP modules along with MiWi network for wireless communication are designed for smart home applications as shown in Figure 5.5.

A regular MiWi Peer to Peer (P2P) protocol application commences by determining the hardware and MiWi P2P protocol. It then tries to launch a connection and permit normal operation mode of receiving and transmitting data. The flowchart for MiWi P2P network is shown in Figure 5.6.

FIGURE 5.5
Prototype of passive infrared (PIR) sensor.

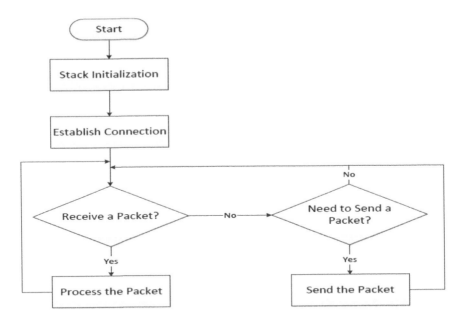

FIGURE 5.6
Flowchart for the MiWi P2P.

The environmental sensor-based procedure has promising method for identifying activities and sensors are used in data collection. Figure 5.7 shows the IoT used in smart healthcare.

The data collected from the sensors by using communication protocols will be handled by the system and smartphone to create activity contexts, such as standing and sitting. Additionally, body sensors are hard to wear, for monitoring all time, in rushing life environment. Here, smartphones are the optional methods for activity recognition as they have benefits of unobtrusiveness and any extra devices are not needed.

The context-aware reasoning system is the major component that gives medical condition valuation (Zhang et al 2018). The remote server and the local client are associated with data analysis and reasoning services.

The first procedure is to collect the sensor data for activity recognition. Mobiles do have the potential to get sensory data and process them.

A Zephyr Bio Harness sensor is used to track trunk movement. Thus, the direction of the phone yields x-axis which is parallel to width as shown in Figure 5.8.

By using the Bluetooth connection, the bio harness data of the sensors are sent to smartphone. The 3D acceleration and orientation of the thigh

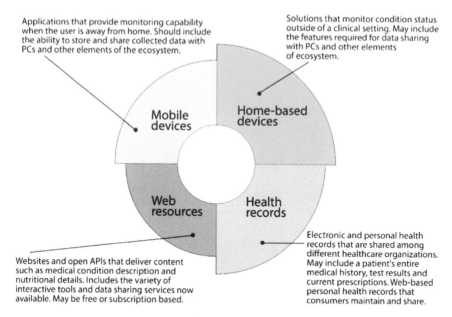

Applications that provide monitoring capability when the user is away from home. Should include the ability to store and share collected data with PCs and other elements of the ecosystem.

Solutions that monitor condition status outside of a clinical setting. May include the features required for data sharing with PCs and other elements of ecosystem.

Websites and open APIs that deliver content such as medical condition description and nutritional details. Includes the variety of interactive tools and data sharing services now available. May be free or subscription based.

Electronic and personal health records that are shared among different healthcare organizations. May include a patient's entire medical history, test results and current prescriptions. Web-based personal health records that consumers maintain and share.

FIGURE 5.7

Internet of Things used in smart healthcare.

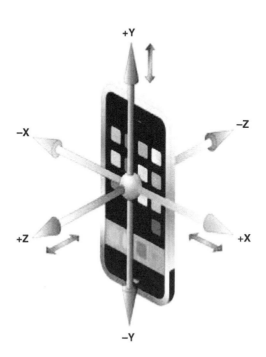

FIGURE 5.8

Body area network for sensor data collection in smartphone 3D acceleration.

and the trunk (t, Ax, Ay, Az, Gx, Gy, Gz, Tx, Ty, and Tz) are gathered with readings of sensor.

If quality needs to be enhanced with sensor readings as shown in Figure 5.9, feature extraction must be applied, when more than one instance is created at any given data point. In order to categorize static and dynamic activities, the standard deviation has to be fixed; henceforth, low irregularity signifies static action and high variability leads to dynamic action.

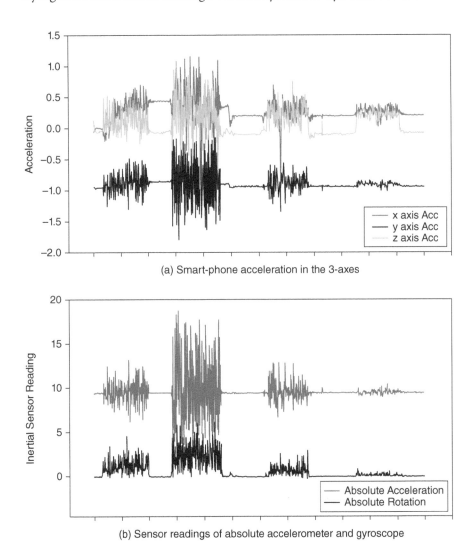

(a) Smart-phone acceleration in the 3-axes

(b) Sensor readings of absolute accelerometer and gyroscope

FIGURE 5.9

Sensor Data of the Phone. (**a**) Smartphone Acceleration in the 3-axes. (**b**) Sensor Readings of Absolute Accelerometer and Gyroscope.

By employing arc cosine conversion given by Equation 5.1, the mean variation over the per second window is given by

$$\alpha_{degrees} = 180 / \pi \ \mathbf{arccos} \ \beta / f \qquad (5.1)$$

where, β is the y-axis mean acceleration, f is the earth gravity, and $\alpha_{degrees}$ is the angle of inclination (Jayalakshmi and Gomathi 2018).

A membership function acts a curve that acts on every element point D in input space diagrammed to a membership value between 0 and 1.

In order to achieve this, provenance-based result tracing approach was employed. This method makes the system reasoning output more useful for the users.

Linguistic rules relate to various fuzzy numbers and sets, which constitute these rules as shown in Table 5.2. The syntax of this rule is: "if x is A then y is B," where x and y are fuzzy numbers in the fuzzy sets A and B, respectively.

The fuzzy sets and rules management are presented in GUI mode as shown in Figure 5.10. This approach also lessens redundancy as well as enhances time efficiency of the rule engine.

The conflicting rules are defined as:

Provided a rule consisting of M fuzzy rules:

$$S_k : \text{if (Dk) then (Bk)} \ 1 <= k <= M$$

S_k and S_p rules are irregular if B_k and B_p conflict each other, then $H_k \wedge H_p$ is not satisfied.

TABLE 5.2

Rules for Generating High-Level Contexts

Medical Context Generating Rules	IF Age is Elderly or Middle Age, and Systolic Blood Pressure is very high, and diastolic Blood Pressure is very high THEN Medical Pre-hypertension.
	IF Systolic Blood Pressure is low and Diastolic Blood Pressure is Low THEN Medical Hypertension.
Event Context Generating Rules	IF On Bed and in Bedroom and Low Activity Level and Light is dark and sound is mute THEN Activity is Sleeping.
	IF TV On and in Living Room and (Low Activity Level or Normal Activity Level) and (Sound is Regular or Loud) THEN Activity is Watching TV.

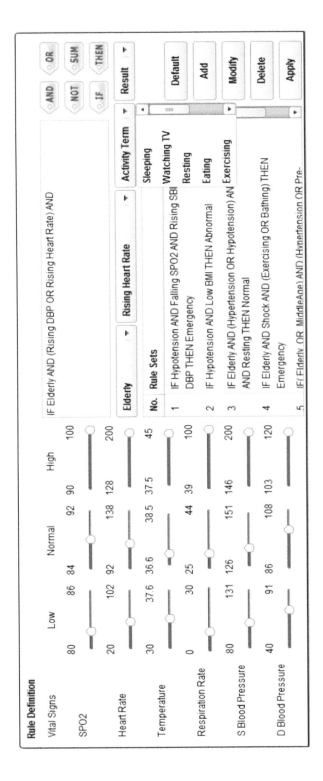

FIGURE 5.10

Fuzzy sets and rules management (Graphical User Interface [GUI] mode).

L_1: if H_k then S_kL_2: if H_p then S_k where $H_p = H_k$. Therefore, either H_k or H_p will be true, S_k is always true.

Whenever irregularity is detected, the fuzzy rule engine tells the user and then gives the liberty to the user to adjust or add any new rules.

5.8 EVALUATION OF THE FRAMEWORK

Remote server and the WSN are used to find the accuracy of the proposed framework. Primarily, the patient can be monitored from Bio Harness sensor.

The following parameters are considered as biomedical parameters:

- Blood pressure
- Body temperature
- Oxygen level
- Heart rate

Here, the parameters are noted with the time duration, ambience, and movement of the patient.

- TP (True Positive) represents abnormality prediction.
- TN (True Negative) represents normal prediction.

The false alarm rate (FP) indicates normal real condition while FN represents abnormality.

Table 5.3 possesses the models such as personal model, default model, and adapted model. The models have been mapped with precision, recall, F-Score, MMC, and Accuracy. It can be seen that the classification accuracy rate of 90% can be observed in Table 5.3. The main reason for achieving accuracy rate of 90% is that all miscellaneous data are terminated, yielding relatively clean data sample. The decision tree classifier finds the best accuracy. The universal model has an accuracy of 80%, which is an average, whereas the personalized model yields 99% and the adapted model provides 93% accuracy (Jayalakshmi and Gomathi 2018).

TABLE 5.3

Classification Accuracy

Classifier	Precision	Recall	F-Score	MMC	Accuracy
Personal Model					
Bayesian Network	98.1	98.2	98.1	98.2	98.1
K-Nearest Neighbor	99	99	99	98.8	99
Neural Network	98.6	98.6	98.6	98.6	98.5
Decision Trees	99	99	99	98.8	99
Default Model					
Bayesian Network	86.2	84.9	85.1	82.1	84.9
K-Nearest Neighbor	97.9	97.9	97.9	97.9	97.9
Neural Network	96.9	97.1	96.9	96.5	96.5
Decision Trees	97.6	97.7	97.8	98.5	97.8
Adapted Model					
Bayesian Network	92.2	94.9	93.1	92.1	93.9
K-Nearest Neighbor	97.9	98.9	97.9	99.5	98.9
Neural Network	98.9	99.1	96.9	96.5	98.5
Decision Trees	98.6	98.7	98.8	98.5	98.5

5.9 CONCLUSION

Healthcare IoT is a set of different IoT technologies and devices used to support personal health, based upon the recorded sensor data. That's the reason the terms healthcare IoT and personal healthcare IoT could be used interchangeably (Zhang et al 2017). Healthcare IoT provides personal services by using personal devices for a single person. Users need a comprehensive system to meet the aims of health monitoring extremely absolute. Accordingly, the appliance must be designed with the end system result in focus. Integration of diagnostic and cure processes is important; therefore, data should be stored in an easy-to-examine-and-transmit format. Decision tree gives the best accuracy of around 90%.

6

Fuzzy Scheduling with IoT for Tracking and Monitoring Hotel Assets

6.1 INTRODUCTION

Revenue management is the optimization of the mix of clients to maximize the revenues, which takes into consideration aspects like rate, length of stay, and arrival and departure dates. Finally, product distribution relates to selling through the most adequate channels which are related to the description of the available profits.

In order to deal with the technophile guest, it is necessary to make the service digitalized. This could convert the service into a digital business model by pushing hospitality services to guests' touchpoint (Tossell 2015). This service platform could provide browsing ability, planning, and picking up of activities by their own self, thus improving the travel experience for the guests.

6.1.1 Smart Hotel

Smart hotel is a systematic process that aims in opening the door, switching on the room lights, and registering a hotel room by pressing a button in our smartphone. Moreover, the smartphone offers novel opportunities for its development and improvement. This particular device could communicate with the hotel server, thus providing access to the controller of the room (Munir et al 2017). It is necessary to have a smartphone with the Android application that could support the smart hotel experience.

The Internet of Things (IoT) plays a major role in the present scenario that has a huge boom toward the hospitality management industry. To play a competitive role in the market, this IoT plays a major role that leads the Hospitality Service Providers (HSP).

The IoT is the interconnection of everyday physical devices like sensors, actuators, identification tags, and mobile devices, so that they could communicate with each other either directly or indirectly through the Internet or any local communication network devices.

This IoT qualifies the normal hotel buildings as a smart hotel that is necessarily present within the smart city. An interaction is produced among the HSP and the guests that could help in collecting the real-time data. This opens up new avenues for immediate, personalized, and localized services as HSP can gauge guest behaviors and preferences with higher accuracy (Adelson 2016).

This also enhances various sectors and departments of HSP by enhancing the back-end efficiency that includes sales, housekeeping, and marketing. This also saves the cost that works with the smart energy management. Figure 6.1 gives the state-of-the-art of a smart hotel.

FIGURE 6.1
State-of-the-art smart hotel.

6.2 PRIOR ART

The system makes use of sensors installed near the user's body and detect the activity that is being performed at a given time. There are smartphones or wearable powered systems that can tell if a hotel worker is walking or running based on his/her movements. However, considering worker's monitoring, the activities that need to be detected depend on the hotel infrastructure, on the monitored worker, and on the field's layout; therefore, it is necessary to have a robust and configurable mechanism according to each farm characteristics.

The ideal sensor locations can choose a wide range of the radios being employed such as, MiWi, as well as the sensitivity of sensors (Turner 2014). Furthermore, wireless sensor networks have evolved into an integral part of the protection of mission-critical infrastructures (Zhong et al 2015).

6.3 UBIQUITOUS COMPUTING

Ubiquitous Computing (UbiComp) is an application of portable computer products in the form of smartphones built into many devices, consequential in a world in which every individual owns and uses many computers. Figure 6.2 depicts the smart room with machine learning technology. Figure 6.3 shows the components of an IoT room

FIGURE 6.2
Machine learning in a smart room.

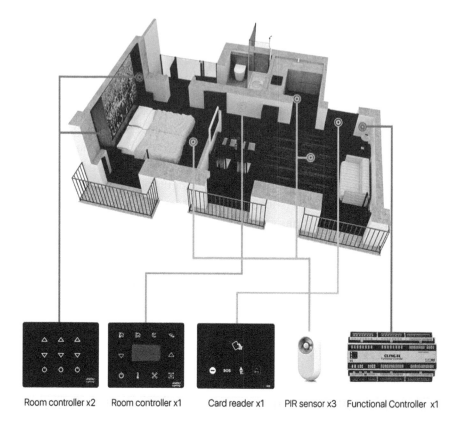

| Room controller x2 | Room controller x1 | Card reader x1 | PIR sensor x3 | Functional Controller x1 |

FIGURE 6.3
Components of IoT rooms.

6.3.1 Hotel Staff Worker's Location Monitoring

In this solution, it was chosen a step-detection approach that searches for acceleration peaks in the worker's movements that have a specific pattern. The real-time coordinates relative to the initial point are calculated based on inertial sensors data (Altin et al 2017). The step-detection process begins in the acceleration amplitude. The acceleration magnitude can be measured by Equation 6.1.

$$\|A\| = \sqrt{A_X^2 + A_Y^2 +}\ A_z^2 \qquad (6.1)$$

One human step makes a peak greater than 13 m/s² in average. Considering the scenario, it defined a 12 m/s² threshold that rejects small worker movements. Here, average step distance can be measured, the azimuth angle and the previous coordinate are the initial points, X and Y will be the positioning of the workers, d is the traveled distance between t-1 and t, represents the azimuth angle and represents the field orientation (Lee and Cheng 2018). The Android gives orientation function that have magnetometer and accelerometer data and finds a vector (Zhong et al 2015).

6.4 SOLUTION DESCRIPTION AND SOLUTION APPROACH

The major applications of Machine Learning algorithm are as follows:

- Abbreviating the measurement cost and accommodation requirements
- Due to the finiteness of training sample sets, coping with the degradation of the classification performance
- Minimizing exploitation and training time
- Promoting data understanding and data conception (Suresh et al 2020)

In world, information is recorded all time. It can be seen; the data evolved at the year 2020 could be 50 times larger than the year 2007. So, it is very necessary to understand data. The data are large, therefore traditional database cannot be used to much extent. Machine learning produces consistent, imitable results (Suresh et al 2020).

There are further two types of classification in supervised learning:

1. Regression
2. Classification

A regression could be used within certain variables for a statistical relationship among two or more variables. Classification arises very commonly in day-by-day life (Turner 2014).

Unsupervised learning examines the instruction even without the utilization of large data in training. A contradiction with supervised learning is that there are no specific goals with each and every input (Suresh et al 2020; Fong et al 2016).

The dimension reduction is just the procedure of declining the amount of random variables of the input without harming any sort of information. Larger amount of input variables and huge data samples result in the raise of intricacy of the dataset. In order to decrease the memory and statistical time, the dimensionality of dataset is decreased. This reduction also helps to abolish unnecessary input variables like replication of variables or variables with a truncated significance level (Jayalakshmi and Gomathi 2018).

Reduction techniques are of two types:

- Feature Selection
- Feature Extraction

6.4.1 Feature Selection

It is the utilization of search engine to obtain the subset of the feature and obtaining the best candidate from the given criteria (Suresh et al 2020).

6.4.2 Feature Extraction

Feature construction, occasionally termed as feature extraction, alludes to transforming the original sample dataset representation by virtue of the process of extracting new features, in order to have the dilemma interpreted in a more discriminative informative space that makes the classification function more proficient (Sotoca and Pla 2010).

By combining several features, these methods transform the feature set into a lower-dimensional feature vector (Ng et al 2008). In this selection, k dimensions are chosen away from d dimensions that provide much information and reject the $(d\text{-}k)$ dimensions. In addition, this selection is also termed as subset selection. The best subset consists of few amounts of dimensions that devote the majority to the accuracy. The finest subset is set up with an appropriate error function.

Data is placed through a definite process of subset production, by using sequential backward selection. The subsequent set is now placed through the procedure to test its performance. If this performance endures the anticipated conditions, then it will be designated as the final subset else the deriving subset will once more be placed through the procedure of subset generation for more fine-tuning.

Feature selection has two different approaches:

- Sequential Forward
- Backward Selection

This sequential forward selection commences a representation which doesn't consist of any predictors, and thereby the predictors are computed to the model, individually till the last predictors. In extracting, at each measurement the variable which provides the maximum supplementary enhancement to the fit is included to the model.

Let us indicate a set by P, which contains the variables Xi, $i = 1,......,d$

$E(P)$ is the error provoked in the test sample.

The sequential forward selection starts with unfilled set with no variables $P = \{\Phi\}$. At every single step, a sole variable is joined to the blank set and a model is skilled, and also the error $E(P \Phi Xi)$ is estimated on test set.

An error condition is placed as per concern, for instance, the meanest square error and misclassification error. From each and every error, the input variable which causes the least error Xj is chosen and combined to the set which is empty P. This model is trained again with the leftover amount of variables and the procedure endures to include variables to P, till the condition $E(P \Phi Xi) < E(P)$.

6.5 RANDOM FOREST

It is a classifier which consists of an accumulation of decision trees, where each and every tree is constructed by employing an algorithm A on the training set S and an extra arbitrary vector, individually as well as equivalently appropriated from certain allocation. The estimation of the random forest is evolved by a maximum vote over the estimations of each and every tree.

The algorithm of the random forest functions are the given by the following procedure:

1. Selects indiscriminate K data points from the guided data.
2. Assembles a decision tree for those particular K data points.
3. Accepts the N tree subset and acts upon step 1 and step 2
4. Determines the division or concludes on the behalf of the superiority of votes.

6.6 NAÏVE BAYES

This particular classifier classifies by using Bayes theorem to categorize the data. This accepts the probability of definite feature X is entirely solitary of the other feature Y. This theorem can be simply demonstrated with the following scenario.

The spanners which are produced by machine A give a probability of 0.6, and the probability of machine B is 0.4. A bug in spanners from the entire assembly is 1%. The probability of damaged spanners generated by machine A is 50% and that of machine B is 50%.

To train the perceptron, subsequent steps are followed:

1. Afford the perceptron with inputs which have a well-known respond.
2. Inquire the perceptron to deduce a respond.
3. Calculate the error.
4. Regulate all the weights with the error, and then go-to step 1 and do again.

This process is repeated until we get the satisfied error. This is the way a single perceptron would function. Then, link all the perceptrons in layers in the input and in the output, in order to produce a neural network. The layers amid the input and the output will be a hidden layer. The application of neuron networks include pattern detection, making prediction, and learning from past data such as biological systems.

The terms neuron or processing element will refer to an operator which maps $R^N\text{->}R$ and is described by Equations 6.2 and 6.3 (Lopes and Ebecken 1997)

$$V_i = G(q_i) = G(a_i c^T + a_{i0})$$

(6.2)

$$V_i = \sum_{j=0}^{N} (a_{ij}c_i + a_{io})$$

(6.3)

Where $c = [c_1, c_2..........,c_N]$ are the input vectors followed by $w_{ij} = [w_{i1}, w_{i2},... ....,w_{iN}]$ which is said to be the weight vectors of N processing elements. It is represented by $G(.)$ that is said to be the monotone function. $G:R^N ->$ (-1,1) or (0,1). Here, it denotes the output in the form of V_i. Artificial neural network is said to be the set of interconnected processing elements. These are formed as layer l=0, 1, 2. L the layer of l determines the input, which is given by the (L-1) layer (Krawczak 2013). Due to this methodology, we call the neural network as feed-forward network. In the current scenario, we use the backward propagation that comes under the concept of supervised neural networks (Suresh et al 2020).

The correction factor could be denoted in the form of Δa_{ij} for the weights a_{ij}, similar to the least mean square algorithm that is equal to $\partial \epsilon_k / \partial a_{ij}(k)$, which denotes the sensitivity factor that could always be negative. The correction factor is shown in Equation 6.4.

$$a_{ij}(k+1)=a_{ij}(k)+u_k\Delta a_{ij}(k)+b_k\Delta a_{ij}(k-1) \qquad (6.4)$$

Where u_k denotes the coefficient of learning factor and $b_k \Delta a_{ij}(k-1)$ is said to be the momentum term.

The concept of self-organization comes under the category of unsupervised learning where we could utilize the training data for detecting the clusters. The internal parameters within the input are compared with the feature map elements and the element that fits into the best match could be the victor. This successful element is taken into consideration and it should be trained further so that these data could be well used and responsive for the accessed input. Kohonen self-organizing feature maps are a supplementary evolvement of the competitive learning. In this case, the best corresponding elements will make their relative element to take part in their training set. This process leads to the similarity of the adjacent elements. In this situation, elements with analogous characteristics could form themselves as a cluster that will map each other and that forms as a feature map, which can be considered as a two-dimensional dataset.

The functionality of the self-organizing map could be denoted by the weights that are initialized to the random variables and the ith mapping element that could vary from k=0, 1, 2, 3,………. Y, as show in the Equation 6.5:

$$\|c(k)-a_c(k)\| = \min\{\|c(k)-w_i(k)\|\} \qquad (6.5)$$

Where, c denotes the best matching pair. During the past years, neural network integrated with the fuzzy-logic combination has been used widely in varieties of application. The natural integration procedure follows both the hybrid neural network with the fuzzy-based systems rather than using a traditional system. They have certain universal and harmonizing activities in common.

The objective of artificial neural network is to detect the abnormal condition and worsening of a mechanical behavior of the equipment. In detecting these habits, the machines have to be trained. This detection has to be declared initially, as the machine will provide the same vibration sign as before a false pattern occurs. Hence, the most sufficient mechanical faults should be evaluated in the beginning. At this particular scenario, the inherent capacity of the generalized neural network could be more suitable. The fault identification could be done by inserting certain malfunction dataset into the trained neural network model that could result in the fault classification pattern. For instance, the dataset of the first and second harmonics of the vibration data could be fed to the machines. If the first harmonics exists in the machine, then the value of imbalance and the probability of misaligned could be detected. Further, if the second harmonics exists then again a value of misalignment and imbalance could be produced which could be analyzed by the neural network.

Data point has no means to relate to another one; it is needed to create a solution to relate small sets of data points that correspond to the execution of an activity. To solve this problem, a dynamic sliding window is used that will aggregate points of physical activity data to feed the classification algorithms.

The solution implements a sliding window algorithm that will apply to the data points of each smartphone sensor (accelerometer, magnetometer, and gyroscope) with a set of statistical operations such as average, minimum, maximum, kurtosis, and standard deviation, for a total of 45 features (3 sensors, 3 axes, 5 statistics). The algorithm starts by reading a total of 150 data points to an array. Each data point has9 points of data, one for each sensor axis. The algorithm calculates the 45 features using the set if statistics previously mentioned one for each axis of each sensor. After calculating the first set of features that will correspond to a point of data on the Data Mining software, the window moves 1.5 seconds (75 data points) to maintain a relation of data with the previous data point. A new data point is then calculated every time the window moves, until all data is processed. In the next step, we use the Weka Library 1, a data mining open-source software to classify the annotated activities. This library has already implemented a set of data classifiers that use machine learning techniques to classify the activities. A pre-evaluation has been done in order to determine which of the algorithms performed the best when classifying the worker's data. From the list of classifiers that were adapted to the type of that we capture with the smartphone sensors, the ones with better performance were BayesNet that implements a Bayes Network and the Multilayer Perceptron which is based on Neural Networks.

On comparing these two algorithms, it is observed that the Bayes Network is faster to create the classification models than Multilayer Perceptron, a known disadvantage of Neural Network algorithms. Despite of that, evaluate the performance of both algorithms while classifying hotel worker activities. The next step is to validate the models created by each classifier. The Weka library presents the results of the learning phase in a confusion matrix and the user has to validate if the values are correctly classified (usually, over 95% of success rate). After this step, the algorithms are ready to classify new activities that were captured from the same worker using the validated classification models.

The first tests to this solution have shown that the classifier algorithms were able to correctly classify with over 90% success rate.

6.7 CONCLUSION

The use of location tracking maps combined with information about the activities that hotel workers perform at a given moment help the hotel management to identify the production process evolution in their performance being able to identify what happens in each area of the field. At this moment, a map with the worker's positioning throughout the day is shown to management combined with a list of the activities they have carried out. In the future this information will be merged in an interactive map where the hotel worker can select a point in the field and view the history from that place, while following which workers passed through the specific place and type of activities that were done.

7

An Effective IoT Drainage System for Detection of Drainage Pipes

7.1 A BRIEF INTRODUCTION TO DRAINAGE SYSTEM

The idea of sustainable development is raising concerns to recreate urban water management (Anguelovski 2016). Sustainable development is that which "meets the requirements and enhances the living conditions of human beings" (Brown et al 2013). The sustainability method concentrates on a situation by implying various concepts in a local area (Capel 2015). The process of gathering man-made and natural information is of prime importance. This chapter is expected to bring out the vital issues such as design, detecting underground drainage pipes and building drainage systems with IoT (Brown et al 2016).

Whenever dry weather happens, water is sent to a water-treatment plant and through wet weather, mixed water ration in combined sewers redirected to receiving area through Combined Sewer Overflows (CSO). When the city is used by a wastewater treatment plant, CSOs might be the major sources of receiving water pollution (De Haan et al 2015). In general, individual systems few times remain almost separate, as some stormwater in foul system and wastewater in storm systems (Furlong et al 2016).

Traditional storm drainage systems consist of many methods that project at restricting the issue as close to the source as possible – thus the term source control (Ahmed et al 2015).

Mostly, the significance of the system improves with the development, yet few exceptions can be found. The understanding about the wet weather pollution potential has quickly amplified nowadays (Byun and Kim 2015).

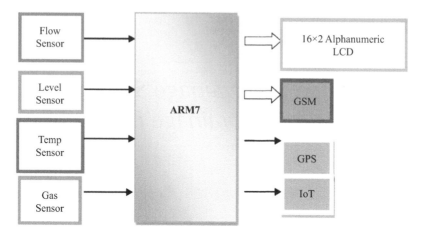

FIGURE 7.1
Drainage system monitoring using IoT devices.

Knowledge about procedure that determines the factor that affects urban storm drainage systems is covered in this chapter. However, this chapter provides latest Internet of Things (IoT) solutions for flooding and water quality problems (Carlson et al 2015). The method of sustainability appeals for enhancements and resources recycling must be considered. Many developed and developing countries invest more on urban drainage system infrastructure (Chesa 2016).

A drainage system monitoring using IoT devices is shown in Figure 7.1.

7.2 INTERNET OF THINGS FOR DRAINAGE SYSTEM

A drainage monitoring system with types of flow, level, gas, and temperature sensors interfaced microcontroller ARM provides effective sustainable development in smarter cities (Cousins 2017). As soon as sensors reach a threshold level, signals from sensors will be sent to microcontroller, (contraindication of that individual value) and sensor forwarded to the microcontroller (Cousins 2017). The water originating from different sources is the primary cause of urban floods such as

FIGURE 7.2
Architecture of IoT sensors for drainage system.

drainage water commencing in the city area water from local rainfall and its connection with the water commencing from the river basin (Moss 2016). The architecture of IoT sensors for drainage system is shown in Figure 7.2.

The water flow sensor consists of water rotor, hall-effect sensor, and a plastic valve. As soon as water flows, the rotor commences its rotation and its rate of flow changes. The pulse signal is based on the output of hall-effect sensor. Drainage system is considered as an integral component of modern infrastructure system; however, the implementation of the drainage system varies in developed countries based on level of development and society awareness. Generally, the effectiveness of drainage system enhances with the level of development with few exceptions (Chesa 2016).

The systems consist of normal function of gathering stormwater and transferring it to the closest point of dumping stormwater. Drainage system is evolving in terms of urban flood protection, pollution control, and management. Drainage systems are commencing to enhance the quality of life by bringing water features such as urban amenity in the city. The flow of isolated foul and surface water drainage is depicted in Figure 7.3.

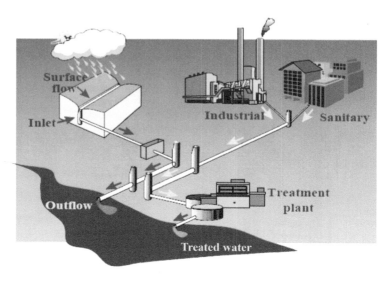

FIGURE 7.3
Flow of isolated foul and surface water drainage.

The complete drainage management system is shown in Figure 7.4. Urban drainage systems are combined with waste and stormwater which consists of a common pipe. When the dry weather commence, water is sent to a treatment plant and when the wet weather commences, a section of the mixed water relates to the sewers separating to receiving stream with the help of the CSOs. In case the city is functioned by a wastewater

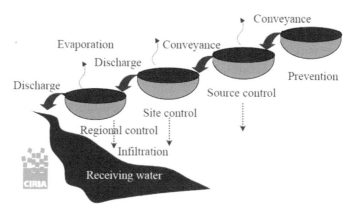

FIGURE 7.4
Drainage management system.

treatment plant, CSOs are considered as an important component for receiving polluted water (Domènech et al 2015).

7.3 BIOSENSORS FOR DRAINAGE SYSTEM WORKERS

Biosensors are bio-factor measurement systems with biological recognition element called probe (also often called as bio-receptor) and a transducer (Vo-Dinh et al 2006). This effect produces during the interaction of analyte with the bio-receptor which is measured by the transducer. The information which is to be extracted is converted into measurable effect like the generation of the electrical signals. Due to this fact, the bio-receptors act as important elements under the biosensor technologies. They permit binding the specific analyte of interest to the sensor for the measurement with minimum interference.

The elements like an enzyme, an antibody, a protein, a living biological system such as cells or tissues, and whole organisms are used for the biochemical mechanism for recognition. For instance, this principle is applied in enzyme reaction in converting the reactant molecule into a product. Sometimes, these enzyme reactions are assisted by using the cofactors. The standard operation of biosensor is shown in Figure 7.5.

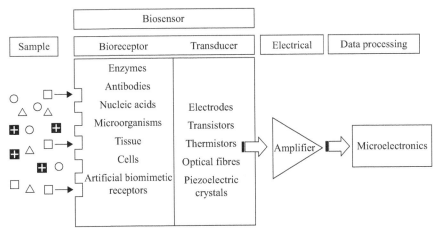

FIGURE 7.5
Standard operation of biosensor.

7.4 GROUND-PENETRATING RADAR (GPR) MAPS FOR DRAINAGE SYSTEMS

7.4.1 Technical Overview

GPR has a greater scope of usage in investigating the thickness of sea ice, identifying ice in permafrost, measuring the thickness and structure of glaciers, locating sewer lines (Drainage lines), cables laid beneath the ground, lakes and rivers bottom proffering, testing the sub-surface of the moon, determining the buried harmful elements in decomposable waste, and also in measuring the scouring around the foundation of various huge structures. The components of GPR system and its interaction are depicted in Figure 7.6

In order to check and locate information from sub-surfaces by the usage of GPR about any medium reduces the effort to a greater extent. Owing to a high resolution and an ability of wide screening and sensing has grown GPR reputation as a non-destructive investigative technique among other available techniques apparently not being widely used.

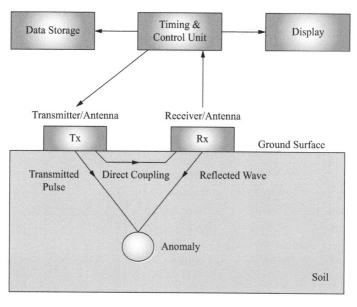

FIGURE 7.6
Components of GPR system and its interaction.

7.4.2 Pipe Penetration

The low-frequency GPR signals penetrate about approximately 1–2 m to the ground level. This figure will vary based on the soil conductivity. The pipe detection is chosen based on the type of pipe and depth of pipe, which is the penetration of pipe in an underground area.

7.4.3 Width of Pipe

The inspection of pipe width covered in the GPR data observations during each view varies with the angle of 3D view. In 3D representation, from the GPR data observations and analyses, the width is not constant. Using this, it becomes possible to inspect almost all GPR data on a single pass with minimum isolation to normal data processing.

7.4.4 Speed of Detection

The shape of the pipe and the dimension of the pipe should detected in less time.

7.4.5 Pipe Detection Capability

This produces an importance to determine the pipe under deep-buried areas, and also in actual site areas in which the noise problems can be avoided. This process detects pipe through synchronized GPR data with proper time-zero position, by tracing the 3D data to a common time-zero position, to align the GPR reflections correctly beneath the objects.

7.5 DRAINAGE PIPE RADIUS DETECTION METHOD

GPR data pipe dimensions' analysis and detection are a major task for GPR designers. This section provides good practice implementation to ensure consistent, efficient, and realistic processing. Techniques used in the proposed work are analyzed by keeping majority synthetic GPR data collected in Software Tool and Surveyed Group Sets, requiring major processing to allow an accurate analysis. The B-scan GPR data is shown in Figure 7.7 and the 3D voxel representation of B-Scan GPR images is shown in Figure 7.8.

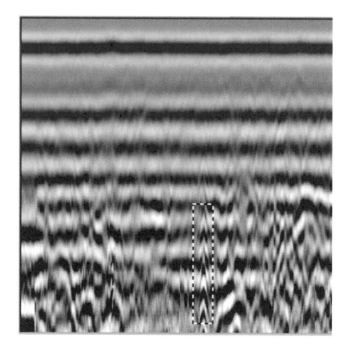

FIGURE 7.7
B-scan of GPR data.

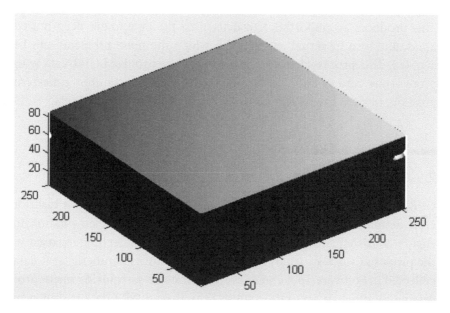

FIGURE 7.8
3D voxel representation of B-Scan GPR images.

FIGURE 7.9
Vertical region of 3D GPR Voxel.

7.5.1 Identify the Regions of 3D GPR Data

To identify the regions of 3D GPR data,

- A very low spatial filter is used to pass these images to reduce the data to a mean level, with the majority of tracing all the regions.
- Place the GPR data within the correct spatial context by repositioning the time zero in the vertical axis.
- Select the gain function for data to exponential gain compensation to emulate the variations in signal amplitude.

Using the above processing steps, the regions of 3D GPR are shown in Figures 7.9, 7.10, and 7.11.

7.5.2 Extraction of Pipe Location

To perform this, analyze the 3D data for region of interest and extract the location of pipe in the pipe view of 3D GPR voxel.

The extraction of pipe location is shown in Figures 7.12–7.19.

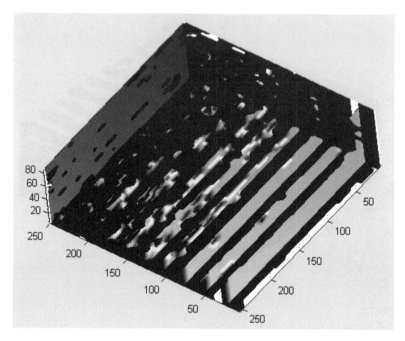

FIGURE 7.10
Horizontal region of 3D GPR Voxel.

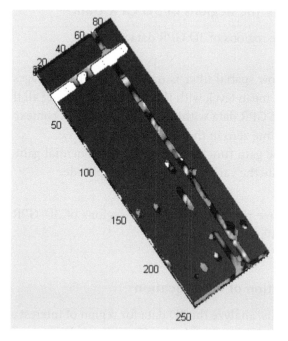

FIGURE 7.11
Pipe view of 3D GPR Voxel.

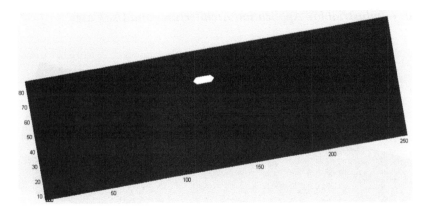

FIGURE 7.12
Pipe location identification.

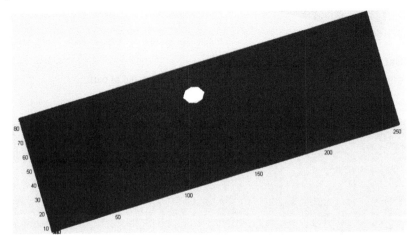

FIGURE 7.13
Pipe location identification by increasing the Π value up to 0.2 of path.

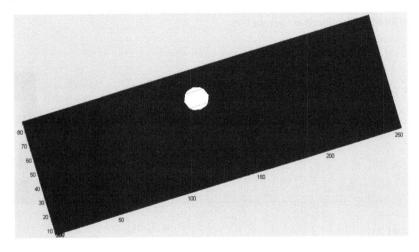

FIGURE 7.14
Pipe location identification by increasing the Π value up to 0.4 of path.

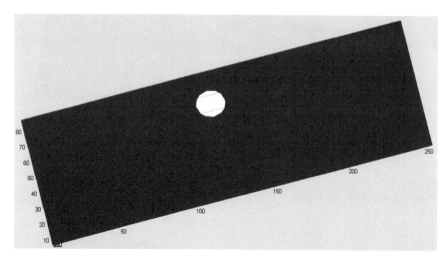

FIGURE 7.15
Pipe location identification by increasing the Π value up to 0.6 of path.

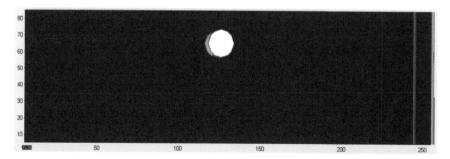

FIGURE 7.16
Pipe location identification in front view.

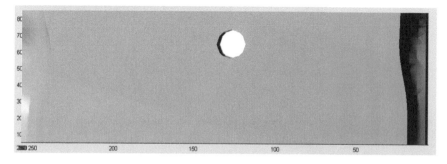

FIGURE 7.17
Pipe location identification in back view.

FIGURE 7.18
Pipe location identification with circle region of interest.

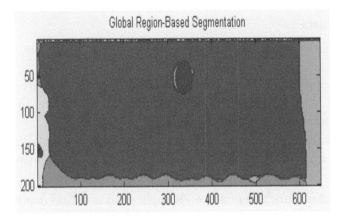

FIGURE 7.19
Pipe location identification with shadow region.

7.5.3 Calculation of Pipe Radius

To calculate the pipe radius, the 3D pipe location and distance measurement is analyzed. The pipe radius detection process is outlined below.

7.5.3.1 Divide the Image

Based on the intensities, the image is divided into different color-based image segmentations. Image threshold is applied on these segments to provide the best choice among the necessary thing (forefront) and the backdrop. Based on the desired level, the threshold takes place due to the conversion of intensity image into a binary image and the obtained value between 0 and 1 concludes the pixels. Set the increment rate up to 0.01 and prefer the finest value to the threshold.

7.5.3.2 Pixel Length Measuring

The hole in the original image is demonstrated by an image segmentation and clean-up procedure, which creates one distinct and cohesive blob. The original image is of binary form which would be enough to build other functions into MATLAB®. This could immediately evaluate the province and a host of diverse information.

7.5.3.3 Pipe Radius

The pipe details are: width = 61 pixels and height = 64 pixels. As shown in Table 7.1, the estimated value was near to the physical measurement on synthetic data.

GPR functionality can be classified in two main modes:

1. Time-of-Flight (ToF): In this scenario, the antennas are placed on land, and imaging is done depending on alterations in electrical properties of the subsurface layers.
2. Drainage system, where one or both antennas are placed in boreholes and topographical subsurface properties are estimated.

The important function of any GPR application is to find depth by penetrating deep into the surface which subsequently depends on the electrical features of the objects hidden and also in which they are surrounded while being buried. The penetration depth is destroyed at a greater pace in conductive loss substances. Because of presence of dissimilar medium, there is a lack of clear reflectors and this is a major factor which limits the functionality of GPR application to determine valid information on the shapes and sizes of structures and also the variety of faults in it. Figure 7.20 shows the analysis of three recorded GPR images.

TABLE 7.1

Tested Pipe Radius Value

Pipe	Width	Height
Synthetic GPR data	0.02 cm	0.03 cm
Real GPR data	0.01 to 0.03 cm (for 61 pixels)	0.02 to 0.03 cm (for 64 pixels)

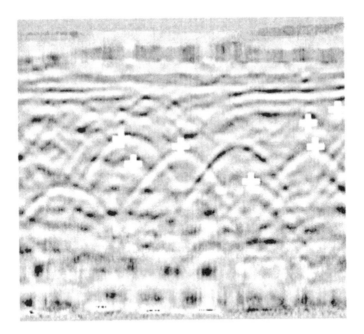

FIGURE 7.20
Analysis of three recorded GPR images.

Various signal establishing ways have been defined to significantly improve the functionality of GPR devices such as wavelets, deconvolution, and spectrogram analysis. Several methods have been developed till date to numerically reproduce and replicate electromagnetic (EM) wave such as ray-based methods, frequency-domain methods, Methods of Moment (MoM), Finite Element Method (FEM), and the Finite-Difference Time-Domain (FDTD) method.

Generally, the penetration depth is higher at lower frequency and varies from about 1 m to 10 m, imaging with high resolution of shallow sub-surface is obtained by using GPR, an EM technique with a frequency between 10 MHZ and 2.5 GHZ. Various sectors that used this technique are militia, study of time and pressure (geology), construction (civil), ice burgs (glaciology), and study of ancient history (archaeology).

A growing number of GPR systems have been reported in recent years on the underground object processing and detection has made deep dwell into the GPR research area. Underground object detection for the geographical surveys and civil aviation have recently become widespread applications in 3D data representation.

To ensure the finer detailed information of GPR data and analyze each and every particle corner of GPR signals, the representation of GPR data becomes a top priority. Several literature surveys have reported these situations. Acting on this situation, 3D model-based designs have developed, which make it possible to detect surface and underground objects with higher speed and precision.

3D model-based designs made actual GPR data survey and analyzed the results to ascertain the underground and buried object properties. With this knowledge, an effective pipe radius detection method is designed. The method utilizes ground penetration radar synthetic and real data images and a synthetic pipe design as an object data acquisition tool. The method relies on using the synthetic data acquisition tool and real-time GPR data to provide an increasingly detailed look at the pipe structure: from 3D appearance to radius measurement.

Among many other object identifications during pipe detection in GPR data, the proposed method has arrived at an analysis of the pipe radius. This analysis has permitted the GPR system to measure the dimensions of underground and buried objects to become the future GPR tools. For the processing of GPR data, scalar migration algorithms developed for 3D seismic data are commonly used. However, the above algorithm does not relate to the GPR transmitter and receiver antennas.

An algorithm takes the data of GPR and these data contain the characteristic of polarization and vectoral radiation. This algorithm is named as multi-component vector imaging algorithm. Polarization of the electric field can be used to reduce unwanted reflections. Polarimetric stepped-frequency GPR and fully polarimetric processing technique have also be developed considering the polarization for GPR detection. Figure 7.21 shows the illustration of GPR survey.

The concept of GPR is widely used in the detection and mapping of data extracted from underground objects like pipes, cables, metals, and so on. The data extracted using GPR is represented in B-scan images and hyperbolic curves. Due to the reflections from objects lying in underground creates a harmonic variation which receives at ground surface located GPR, displays the regions of objects with the effects of cross-section, area, segments, and impedance. The collected data are displayed in B-scan to analyze the reflections in the shape of hyperbolic curves. Contribution on this research work has developed different strategies to extract the features

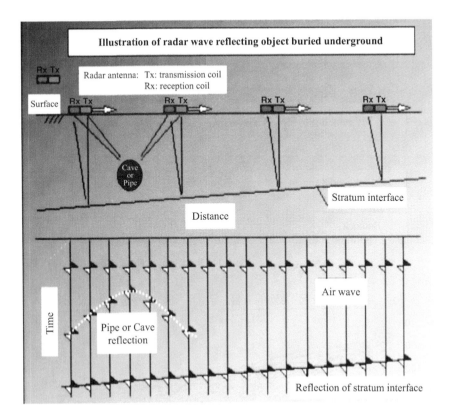

FIGURE 7.21
Illustration of GPR survey.

of GPR data. The various applications of GPR technique are described in Figures 7.22–7.26.

It is noted that lack of GPR leads to the higher conductivity of contaminated water.

Detection of landmines, pipes, specific objects, water compounds, material compounds, and many structures underground by GPR has been developed by various researchers, underneath several applications essentially in civil engineering, archaeology, and geology. To align on these to cover object classification and detection, several computer-aided systems have been successfully developed. These models classify the object based on features, coefficients, and plane distributions. Pipe STL 3D data are transported to MATLAB automatically by using ASCII array (Peng et al 2020).

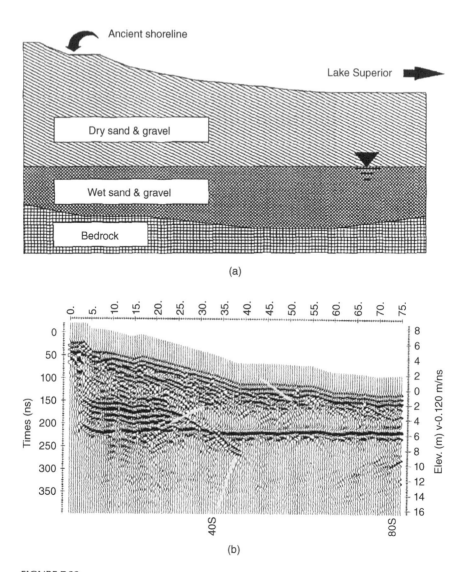

FIGURE 7.22

(a) and (b) Employing GPR for mapping groundwater-surface and sand/gravel bedrock interface.

Feature extraction of pipe 3D data is classified into individual plane using first and second models. After first and second model feature extraction, features STL data are processed by visualization algorithm stated, using an open-source visual algorithm 3D model-based computer-aided application.

FIGURE 7.23
An application of GPR used for detecting underground services.

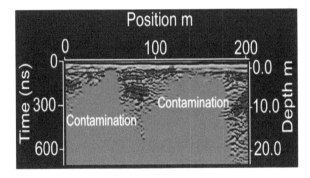

FIGURE 7.24
Radar section of an area of contaminated water.

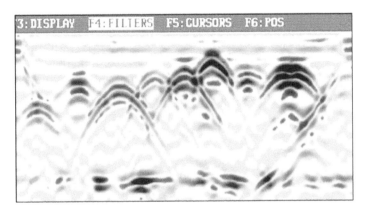

FIGURE 7.25
GPR is used to determine the various items made up of different materials at depth.

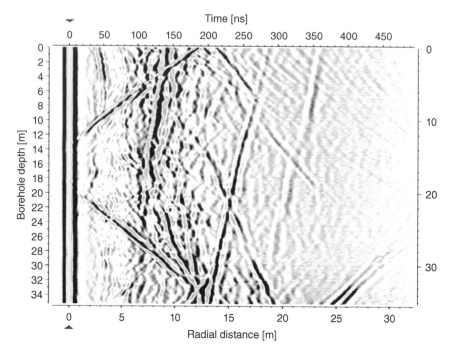

FIGURE 7.26
A GPR image used in drainage hole system radar.

7.6 CONCLUSION

This chapter describes the scenario in developing counties changes rapidly in the sense where all parties take role in planning, design, management and maintenance and well funding are getting aware that storm drainage must be in consideration. On the other side, it must be implemented into urban infrastructure projects with their mutual interactions encircling not only the conventional problem of flood mitigation and health hazard reduction (water quality concerns) and challenges of urban infrastructure and resources management.

8

Predictive Maintenance in IoT for Retail Machine Industries

8.1 INTRODUCTION

Retailers have started to integrate IoT technologies to achieve a true omni-channel experience by getting digital to retail stores (Al-Fuqaha et al 2015). People must be given an option of interacting with retailers in different channels, by using mobile devices in retail location-based functionality.

New e-Commerce-driven competitors have high costs and lesser margins, and retailers aim at a major goal to improve efficiency for their business processes (Andersson and Mattsson 2015). Sensors, cameras, beacons, and Wi-Fi networks will get valuable information which will be analyzed (Balaji and Roy 2017). Retailers construct sufficient infrastructure for a network and analytics tools to get benefit of various offer IoT solutions (Barratt et al 2015).

IoT in smart retail vendor machines is shown in Figure 8.1.

Large retail chains are actively spending in IoT technologies, and retailers found its applicability for their company (Bello et al 2015). Projects get bigger slowly, and do not need investment as software can be devoted fully as a service. Figure 8.2 shows the global data survey.

IoT can also improve people's experience in provisions by interactive terminals. Additionally, targeted messages will be on digital screens based on customers' gender (Brody and Pureswaran 2015). Figure 8.3 illustrates IoT in retail.

FIGURE 8.1

IoT in smart retail vendor machines.

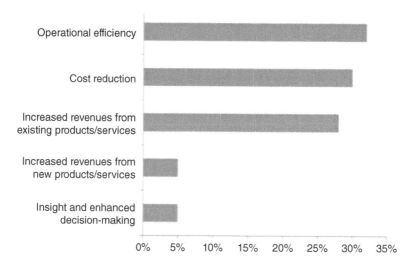

FIGURE 8.2

Global data survey.

FIGURE 8.3
IoT in retail.

8.2 DEAD RECKONING FOR LOCATING EMPLOYEE AND CUSTOMER MOVEMENT FOR SMART RETAIL INDUSTRIES

Dead Reckoning is a direction-finding technology capable to remove relative displacements to a before identified position by observing user's movements (Dasgupta et al 2016).

To measure displacements to the initial position, it is used as an inertial navigation technique based on inertial sensors data available on smartphones such as accelerometers and magnetometers. With this sensor, it is possible to give the device a direction at any given time.

There are two types of Dead Reckoning:

1. Acceleration integration
2. Step's counting

The first method is based on the fact that distance is given by integrating velocity over time and velocity is given by integrating acceleration over time.

Smartphone sensors are very inaccurate and the integration process expands the error with calculated distances being different from the real-walk distances. The second method is to calculate the total acceleration on the device and search for peaks over the time that are likely to be steps (over *13m/s²*). In this process, the gravity of Earth must be considered for appropriate result. Knowing the person's average step length, it is then calculated the new relative position to the initial points (Dijkman et al 2015). A Pedestrian Dead Reckoning system to monitor user's indoor positioning uses a regular smartphone. A sample of the acceleration caused by a customer/hotel worker in a hotel is shown in Figure 8.4.

This system makes use of the built-in accelerometer to detect and estimate the next position. The first one is static and works by multiplying the person's height with a predetermined constant K, which is equal to 0.415 for men and 0.413 for woman. They also present three other methods that are dynamic and take into the account the accelerations when walking. The method with best results has a medium error of 1.39 m to a traveled distance of 30 m. To detect the steps, the authors use a detection method that searches for peaks in acceleration amplitude, as opposed to peaks in vertical acceleration where it is needed to tackle the smartphone rotation problem.

Predictive maintenance is a method, which consumes the direct monitoring of mechanical condition of plant equipment to decide the actual mean time to malfunction for each preferred machine (Feretti and Schiavone 2016). Predictive maintenance helps in predicting things before they happen in the environment (Firdausi 2016). The smart retail gateway machines are depicted in Figure 8.5.

Signature analysis is the most commonly used vibration methods. It is possible by implementing this analysis; it can predict the mechanical condition of the machines. Yet, there is a constraint that this particular analysis method cannot be used for the estimation of the mechanical failure. In prediction, best statistical model will be chosen to achieve the right insight of data from information (Gerpott and May 2016). The hidden pattern disclosed by a process could make us to find the prediction. It can be used in manufacturing as well as retail industries as the customers can be impressed with desired results.

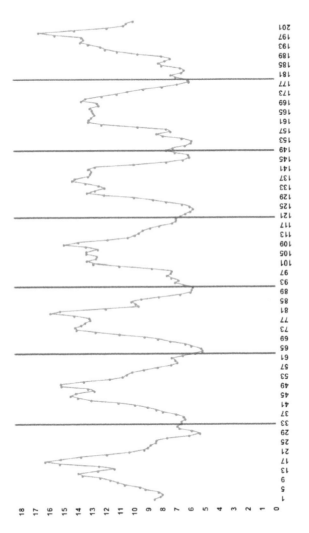

FIGURE 8.4

Sample of the acceleration caused by a customer/hotel worker in a hotel.

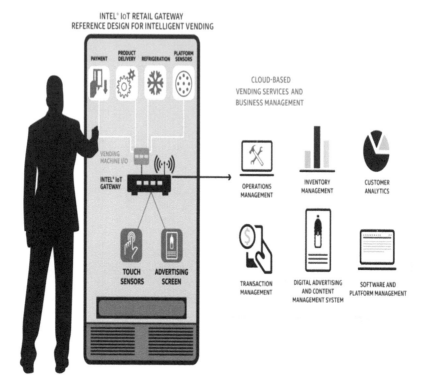

FIGURE 8.5
Smart retail gateway machines.

The steps involved in this process are:

1. Collect data
2. Clean data
3. Identify patterns
4. Make predictions

Predictive modeling and analysis help in development of their quality with appropriate decision =. Every organization uses the customers' social media data to find the best out of them.

8.3 PRIOR ART

Inspite of the achievement of integrated predictive analytics by business, information systems researchers (Suresh et al 2019).

8.4 CASE STUDY

8.4.1 Predictive Machines Best Methods for Smarter Retail

In the Statistical Process Control (SPC), accurate data will help us in a proactive control process and turn away the quality of producer malfunction before happening (Kshetri 2017).

For example, a customer wants to purchase a product. He/she identifies a fault in that product and conveys the plant manager about the issue. Then, the organization must take action if the information given by the customer is genuine (Suresh et al 2019).

8.5 SOLUTION DESCRIPTION AND APPROACH

Manufacturers focus more on the product quality. Still it needs to find optimal functioning with finest creation potential (Lee and Lee 2015). With predictive analytics, we can find the better quality and high Return on Investment (ROI) (Suresh et al 2019).

The predictive analysis has benefits like it also checks the possible routes within the company to save the industry (Manyika et al 2015).

8.6 EXHIBIT PROFILES FOR AN INTELLIGENT MACHINE WITH SMART RETAIL

The prescriptive analytics, on the other hand, is related to making certain predictions regarding the equipment that it could happen in the near future (Murray et al 2016). Hence, the results are being completed that concludes with activities where decision producer can take decisions (Newe 2015). The Exhibit Profiles for an intelligent machine with smart retail is shown in Figure 8.6.

Machine learning algorithm is a widely used classification algorithm, which is used in various fields. Many algorithms have been employed (Nolin and Oslon 2016), which are compared with the classification accuracy of classifiers reliant on words to that of classifiers based on senses. Naive Bayes are employed in text classification applications and it is

Exhibit Profile

Application and Management Software	Self-service, Kiosk, Vending	Visual Marketing	Intelligent Identification Systems	Smart Payment Systems
• Intelligent Marketing • Retail Solutions • Member Management Systems • APP • Cloud Data Analysis • Communication Services • Multimedia Exhibition Halls	• Queuing Systems • POS Machines • Touch Kiosks • Vending Machines • Bill Printing • Interactive Terminals	• Illumination • Advertising equipment • 3D Glass-Free Displays • Display Terminals • LCD Advertising Players • Virtual Fitting Rooms • POP	• Bar Code Recognition • Techniques • RFID • Facial Recognition • Biometric Identification • Identity Recognition	• Mobile Payment • Online Payment • NFC Payment • Card Reader Systems • Stylus Printing

FIGURE 8.6
Exhibit profiles for an intelligent machine with smart retail.

widely used, its simplicity and effectiveness are its important features. Classification works based on their characteristics and their nature. The commonly used data mining functionalities are Association Analysis, Characterization and Discrimination, Classification, and Prediction.

Machine learning algorithms are the key factors for driving the data from the prediction and failure detection using certain algorithms that could be either data analysis or statistical techniques. For the generation of this data-driven model, it could be obtained by these data records and outputs that occur through the historical data of these predictive models constructed into its training stage (Palattella et al 2016). For the decision-making, the test data could be appraised through this model. The conclusion made by this decision analysis could be the predicted data either regarding the asset of the industries or the prediction of event and the type of breakdown. In certain industries, the management team uses robots for this job, which could adapt easily for such a detection thus providing a safe environment to the industries. These industrial robots are said to be the manipulators that are created to shift the parts and substances, which could perform various task in certain way that it has been programmed. Due to the mechanical part arrangement and their control system technologies used, certain reasons could be accredited to malfunction in these robots (Pang et al 2015). These failures could be in the form of any brake malfunction or any sort of repair in the electrical motors used in the robots for their movements. This could result in the short circuit. When a single model is used as a fault detection framework, then these types of faults couldn't be bought under a single evolution and it couldn't be very easy to combine. To negotiate this, the technique of data-driven models have been used.

A machine learning tool into certain failure mode considered and bought a technique for estimating independent system routine dependability in realtime. This technique involves online monitoring of multiple variables and brings out the performance of the systems thus estimating their reliable performing condition. This was bought in various time series as a multivariable state-space approach. In order to obtain the reliability of the system, the estimated covariance matrix and the mean vectors are taken into consideration.

Through this developed system, it is possible to anticipate and calculate the function deprivation of each and every structure in a vibrant surroundings in realtime. To predict the engine condition, the artificial neural network (ANN) algorithms have been used. They also made diagnosis and extrapolative technologies that made a set of integrated turbo machinery supervising. This type of machine could be fitted in the aircraft that uses the turbo machinery for the middle-sized pumps to the ground-based gas engines. This resulted in the noteworthy perspective for the reduction of current cost.

Moreover, neural networks play a major role in certain field that could help in improvised operating systems in the realtime. Several sensors have to be implemented in this field for the detection of certain vibration in the machines. These sensors' output could be fed as the input to these neural network algorithm. According to Kumar et al (2016), neural networks could be used in the field of hydroelectric power plants and the replacement of components in the surface mount technologies (Suresh et al 2020).

Supervised learning possesses regression and classification. Substantially, it contains partitioning up objects. Each object is accredited to one of a number of mutually exhaustive and exclusive kinds known as classes. Each object should be authorized to specifically one class, i.e., more than one object shouldn't be attached to a single class. Unsupervised learning examines how systems could acquire to signify meticulous input patterns in a path that redirects the statistical structure of the general collection of input patterns (Suresh et al 2020).

A contradiction with supervised learning is that there are no specific objective outputs or environmental estimation accompanying with each and every input. This reduction is just the procedure of declining the amount of random variables of the input without harming any sort of information. Larger amount of input variables and huge data samples result in the raise of intricacy of the dataset. In order to decrease the memory and statistical time, the dimensionality of dataset is decreased. This reduction also helps to abolish unnecessary input variables like replication of variables or variables with a truncated significance level.

Filtering methods such as bilateral information, autonomous component analysis, class detaching measure, or variable ranking could be effectively used for classification (Suresh et al 2020). Feature construction, occasionally termed as feature extraction; allude to transforming the original sample dataset representation by virtue of the process of extracting new features, in order to have the dilemma interpreted in a more discriminative informative space that makes the classification function more proficient (Sotoca and Pla 2010). By combining several features, these methods transform the feature set into a lower-dimensional feature vector (Ng et al 2008).

Extraneous and redundant features are discarded by supervised feature selection that arbitrates relevant features by their affiliation with the corresponding class labels. In this selection, k dimensions are chosen away from d dimensions that provide much information and reject the $(d-k)$ dimensions. In addition, this selection is also termed as subset selection. The best subset consists of few amounts of dimensions that devote the majority to the accuracy. The finest subset is set up with appropriate error function.

Sequential forward selection commences a representation which doesn't consist of any predictors, and thereby the predictors are computed to the model, individually till the last predictors. In exacting, at each measurement the variable which provides the maximum supplementary enhancement to the fit is included to the model. Let us indicate a set by P, which contains the variables X_i, $i = 1,......, d$ and $E(P)$ is the error provoked in the test sample. An error condition is placed as per concern, for instance, the mean square error and misclassification error. From each and every error, the input variable, which causes the least error X_j, is chosen and combined to the set which is empty P. This model is trained again with the leftover amount of variables and the procedure endures to include variables to P, till the condition $E(P \Phi X_i) < E(P)$. Sequential backward selection is an effective substitute for the most excellent subset solution. But, it starts with an occupied set of features contrasting sequential forward selection. It eliminates the minimum significant features each at an instance iteratively. The selection begins with a packed set of variables $P = \{1,2,3,....,d\}$. At every single step, the model is skilled with a complete set of variables and the error is calculated in test set. The variable with the maximum error Xj is detained from the set P. The model is qualified once more with a novel set of variables P, and the step extends to eliminate variables from P, till the condition $E(P-Xj) <E(P)$.

8.7 INTELLIGENT RETAILER MACHINES WITH MACHINE LEARNING ALGORITHMS

8.7.1 Random Forest

The estimation of the random forest is evolved by a maximum vote over the estimations of each and every tree. The algorithm of the random forest functions is given below:

1. Select indiscriminate K data points from the guided data.
2. Assemble a decision tree for those particular K data points.
3. Accept the N tree subset and acts upon steps 1 and 2.
4. Determine the division or conclude on behalf of the superiority of votes.

8.7.2 Naïve Bayes

This particular classifier classifies by using Bayes theorem to categorize the data. This accepts the probability of definite feature X is entirely solitary of the other feature Y. This theorem can be simply demonstrated with the following scenario.

The spanners which are produced by machine gives a probability of 0.6, and the probability of machine B is 0.4. A bug in spanners from the entire assembly is 1%. The probability of damaged spanners generated by machine A is 50% and that of machine B is 50 %. In this particular example, Bayes theorem can be used to reply what is the probability of defects generated by machine B.

8.7.3 AdaBoost

Boosting is an amalgamation method which is used for constituting extremely precise estimation or durable classifier from comparatively scrawny and imprecise classifiers. This algorithm is a process of iteration where a model is skilled in data and estimates frail learners. The next model skills itself from the errors which it makes from the prior training and stick to the errors and the progression endures till the data are properly estimated. Correctly classified samples are weighted low by multiplying with *e*QTS and the misclassified samples are weighted further by multiplying with *e*QTS and finally all weights are normalized to 1. Currently, the next model is trained G2 and the similar procedure persists till best possible samples are suitably classified and last model is the addition of every weighted models.

The foremost set of self-determining predictor variables which are to be modeled is training sample. Subsequent to the achievement of the modeling error rate, the feeble learners are identified. Those novice feeble learners are weighted and the samples are once again modeled and these procedures persist up to M number of times and at last all the outputs from various samples are averaged to produce the boosted output. Each and every input which is received by a neuron must be slanted, i.e. multiplied by some value. Generating a perceptron usually starts by conveying random weights. Every input is taken individually and multiplied by its weight. The generation of the output takes place by transferring the sum throughout an activation function. If it is a simple binary output, then activation function tells whether the perceptron is to be "fired" or not. For instance, if the sum is positive number, then 1 will be the output; if the sum is negative, then –1 will be the output. Additional factor to be considered is bias. If both the inputs are equal to zero, then any sum would be zero which is independent of multiplicative weight.

To end this particular problem, a third input is summed which is called as the bias input with a value of 1. This process is repeated until we get the error in which we are satisfied. This is the way a single perceptron would function. Then, we have to link all the perceptrons in layers in the input and in the output, in order to produce a neural network.

ANN is said to be the set of interconnected processing elements. These are formed as layer l=0, 1, 2, ... L. The layer of l determines the input, which is given by the (L-1) layer. Due to this methodology, we call the neural network as feed-forward network. In the current scenario, we use the backward propagation that comes under the concept of supervised neural networks (Suresh et al 2020).

The correction factor could be denoted in the form of Δa_{ij} for the weights a_{ij}, similar to the least mean square algorithm that is equal to $\partial \epsilon_k / \partial a_{ij}(k)$, which denotes the sensitivity factor that could be always negative. The concept of self-organization comes under the category of unsupervised learning where we could utilize the training data for detecting the clusters. The internal parameters within the input are compared with the feature map elements and the element that fits into the best match could be the victor. This successful element is taken into consideration and it should be trained further so that these data could be used well and be responsive for the accessed input.

Kohonen self-organizing feature maps are a supplementary evolvement of the competitive learning. In this case, the best corresponding elements will make their relative element to take part in their training set. This process leads to the similarity of the adjacent elements. In this situation, the analogous characteristics elements could form themselves as a cluster that maps each other. The set that forms as a feature map, could be considered as a two-dimensional data set. The objective of ANN is to detect the abnormal condition and worsening of a mechanical behavior of the equipment. In detecting these habits, the machines have to be trained. This detection has to be declared at a first sign itself, since the machine could provide the same vibration sign as before that could give a false pattern of the malfunction (Gungor V.C. and F. C. Lambert). Hence, the most sufficient mechanical faults should be evaluated at the first itself. At this particular scenario, the inherent capacity of the generalized neural network could be more suitable.

The fault identification could be done by inserting certain malfunction dataset into the trained neural network model that could result in the fault-classification pattern. For instance, the dataset of the first and second harmonics of the vibrational data could be fed to the machines. If the first harmonic exists in the machine then the value of imbalance and the probability of misaligned could be detected. Further, if the second harmonics exists then again a value of misalignment and imbalance could be produced which could be analyzed by the neural network.

8.8 MONITORING SMART RETAIL MACHINES

This section is completely regarding the monitoring of the machine. Suppose, if we fit the vibrational sensor in the machine then these data have to be validated. This could be done by the data acquisition system. The data acquisition system is nothing but a board that could convert the analog values coming from the transmitter into a digital format. It could be monitored with 256 channels that could be connected with eight machines. This could generate the alarm data when certain abnormal circumstances occur.

With the help of trend analysis, we can determine the maximum risk factors that could occur in the machines of the industry. For this evaluation, we could use certain measurement dataset concerning to the measured points of the machine. With the help of regression curves, we infer the particular operating system so that the alarm is reached. These set of variables could be predefined by the operators. Predictive maintenance will be really effectual if interpretation regarding the vibration development beside the time is accomplished. Prediction is the difficulty of drawing calculations regarding known time series into the future. Hybrid neural network is nothing but a combination of fuzzy logic system that could be helpful in making a certain decision. The fuzzy system is really helpful for making a certain decision. It uses the normal IF-THEN statement for its decision. The combination of fuzzy system in the ANN helps us in providing a crisp output. The input data determined by the machines could be evaluated through the fuzzy logical system to produce a crisp input. This in turn combines with certain decision-making statement and filters out itself with the logical and necessary data. This filtered fuzzy data are send to the process of Defuzzification, where the fuzzy input data produce themselves to become crisp output data.

It is proved that ANN and IoT form the greatest of all algorithms. The next lies the SVM (Support Vector Machines). In SVM model, the training/test samples are represented as dot/points in the space and they are mapped in such a way that the clear gap among the categories appears which separates the samples. New test samples/examples are later mapped on the using the kernel trick SVMs are also be able to perform non-linear classification in addition to linear classification. SVM helps to build hyper plane in any space and can be used on tasks such as regression, prediction, or classification.

8.9 CONCLUSION

The IoT implementations value lies in the analytics capabilities at the backend and the can combine various data sources for making correlations and high accuracy. The need to model many complicated functions with the same idea gave rise to the concept of ANN. The technique behind learning is that interactively determining the coefficients for the input and the output that lead to the prediction. For the function approximation as stated in the previous sentence, it is not necessary for the neural network to fit into a straight line. But for the ANN, any shape or a curve could be fitted. The extension of the function approximation arises the forecasting that could predict the time series data. We have a target variable and if that value predicts the same point in the future time then at each step of the training phase we should present with the historical data to the neural network. For instance, 60th week dataset had to be fed which is asked to estimate the 61st week based on the time series. This could be best done by ANN. This type of analysis is done at the stock market where it is necessary to detect the share values (which entirely runs on the basis of prediction). ANN and IoT work well with the sample classification that maps the input data with the various categories and classes. With ANN, it could be really easy to cluster the classified records. Higher output nodes with an input react more effectively for that sample.

9

Integrating ANN and IoT for Predictive Maintenance in Industries

9.1 INTRODUCTION

The main objective of prediction is needed in health monitoring as it helps in continuously monitoring the health of a patient and there is no need for any person to be with the patient (Annamalai and Udendhran 2019).

Pervasive healthcare has two categories:

1. Pervasive computing tools
2. Enabling it throughout the time (Annamalai, Udendhran and Vimal 2019)

The main aim of predictive maintenance is to focus on condition monitoring. Condition-based monitoring is the analysis of a machine without interrupting its original work. Additionally, condition monitoring of equipment is one of the decision-making strategies that can avoid any type of faults that can occur in the near future.

Prognostic Health Monitoring (PHM) is analyzing the feature possibilities that could occur for the patient. As per the estimation, about 20–30% of the periodically monitored equipment for predictive maintenance has been affected from its production and its quality has to be examined regularly (Annamalai et al 2019). The monitoring the equipment in a weekly or monthly manner does not prove to be enough for detecting certain abnormalities in the machines (Ettlinger and Gordon 2011). If equipment changes from periodical to continuous monitoring then it could lower the cost of expenditure for the machines considerably (Annamalai and Udendhran 2019).

Manufacturing analytics

Costs
- Waste rates
- Inventory turns
- Value-added analysis
- Cost productivity
- Overhead efficiency
- System complexity

Finance

Human Resources

Production quality
- Vendor quality
- Production quality
- Data accuracy
- Cost of quality

Operations

Manufacturing organization

Lead times
- Cycle times
- Setup times
- Material availability
- Machine uptime
- Customer service time

Sales and Marketing

Research

Delivery reliability
- Vendor delivery performance
- Schedule adherence
- Order and schedule changes
- Lost sales

FIGURE 9.1
Manufacturing industry quality and analysis.

9.2 APPLICATION

It consumes direct monitoring of mechanical condition of plant equipment to decide the actual meantime of malfunction for each preferred machine (Dumitrache and Caramihai 2010; Annamalai and Udendhran 2019; Annamalai et al 2019). The information could be generated before any hazardous situation could occur in the equipment.

Key role in search marketing and commendation engines is shown in Figure 9.1.

Every organization will have a statistical analysis of its data and can analyze its environment well at certain limits like turnover activities, total number of clients, follow the supplies, and so on.

9.3 KNOWLEDGE REGARDING THE PREDICTION OF SUITABLE OPPORTUNITY

If there is a defect in the product, when the customer is informing about it, then it should be taken into account, considering the user's request.

Thereafter, if it's genuine then the necessary actions can be taken for the case so that it does not happen in the upcoming days.

9.4 MAINTENANCE OF THE BEST PRACTICES

It is necessary to make adjustments in the wide range of enterprise by having maintenance over the entire project instead of using own plant (Annamalai and Udendhran 2019).

Using predictive analytics, it is feasible to get the better quality of manufacture, Return on Investment (ROI) and Overall Equipment Effectiveness (OEE), brand's status, and ensures the safety of the customer (Annamalai et al 2019). The advantages of this approach are:

- Minimization of downtime cost
- Minimization of the production loss
- Reduction of manual work
- Revenue maximization
- Improvement of employee's maintenance

9.5 ANALYTICS BACKGROUND

Variations in these analytical models are categorized as

- Descriptive,
- Prescriptive, and
- Predictive.

9.5.1 Descriptive Analytics

It collects, organizes, tabulates, and depicts the data where it cannot provide the user with information regarding occurrences of event or regarding the happenings in the near future.

9.5.2 Prescriptive Analytics

It is related to making certain predictions regarding the equipment that could happen in the near future which is clear and precise

9.5.3 Predictive Analytics

It is for analyzing the near-future happenings and events. Also, if it may cause bad effects then it has to be stopped at once.

These have produced a report regarding the intelligence-based predictive modeling that is shown in Figure 9.2.

Machine learning algorithm is widely used for classification algorithm in various fields of applications like healthcare, education, and so on. Naive Bayes are employed in text classification applications and these are widely used. Their simplicity and effectiveness are their important features. Schneider presented the problems encountered and also provided solutions fort the existing problems.

Machine learning algorithms are the key factors for driving the data from prediction and failure detection using certain algorithms that could be either data analysis or statistical techniques. The generation of this data-driven model could be obtained by data records and outputs that

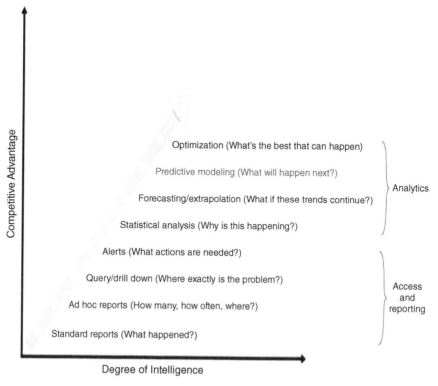

FIGURE 9.2
Predictive analysis with the degree of intelligence.

occur through the historical data of these predictive models that are constructed into its training stage.

For the decision, the test data could be appraised through this model The conclusion made by this decision analysis could be the predicted data either regarding the asset of the industries or the prediction of event and the type of breakdown.

Due to the mechanical part arrangement and their control system technologies used, certain reasons could be accredited to malfunction in these robots. These failures could be in the form of any brake malfunction or any sort of repair in the electrical motors used in the robots for their movements (Gandino and Montrucchio 2013).

This could result in a short circuit. When a single model is used as a fault-detection framework, then these types of faults could not be brought under a single evolution and are not very easy to combine. To negotiate this, we use the technique of data-driven models. In order to obtain the reliability of the system, the estimated covariance matrix and the mean vectors are taken into consideration.

Through this developed system, we could anticipate and calculate the function deprivation of each and every structure in a vibrant surroundings in real time. Atzori et al (2010) made a model for calibration and prophetic equipment for the turbines (gas engine). To predict the engine condition, the artificial neural network (ANN) algorithms are been used. Moreover, neural networks play a major role in certain fields that could help in improvised operating systems in the real-time as shown in Figure 9.3. Several sensors have to be implemented in this field for the detection of certain vibration in the machines.

These sensor output could be fed as the input to these neural network algorithms. Neural networks could be used in the field of hydroelectric power plants and the replacement of components in the surface-mount technologies (Kumar et al 2016).

9.6 SOLUTION APPROACH

This chapter delineates fundamental feature selection issues and current research objectives. Machine learning is an evolving field today due to an increase in number of data. It aids to progress observations from a huge quantity of data which were very ponderous to humans and at times also inaccessible (Suresh et al 2020).

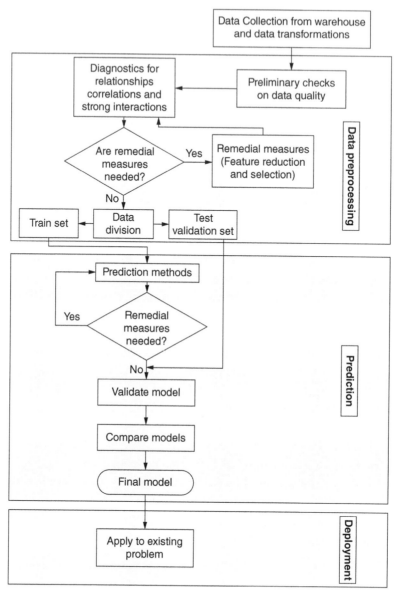

FIGURE 9.3
General process in the artificial neural network.

The prime applications of feature selection are as follows:

1. Abbreviating the measurement cost and accommodation requirements
2. Due to the finiteness of training sample sets, it enables coping with the degradation of the classification performance

3. Minimizing exploitation and training time
4. Promoting data understanding and data conception. It may be visualized that evaluating the significance of distinctive description may not be crucial; nevertheless, the actual remonstrance is to evaluate the consequence of subsets of features (Suresh et al 2020).

Evaluating data or constructing extrapolative models by hand is almost unfeasible in some consequences, and also consumes more time and takes away productivity. Machine learning, produces consistent, imitable results, and educates itself from previous computation of data sets.

After gaining the set of data, algorithms simplify the data and articulate the refutable value H for the given sets of data

---

9.7 DIMENSION REDUCTION TECHNIQUES

This reduction is just a procedure of declining the amount of random variables of the input without harming any information. This reduction also helps to abolish unnecessary input variables like replication of variables or variables with a truncated significance level. These reduction techniques are of two types namely: Feature Selection and Feature Extraction.

9.7.1 Feature Selection

This particular framework is comprised of two parts:

1. Utilization of search engine to obtain the subset features and obtaining the best candidate from the given criteria. The inspection for a variable subset is a NP-hard enigma.

   In this selection, k dimensions are chosen from d dimensions that provide much information and reject the $(d-k)$ dimensions (Suresh et al 2020).
2. Training the data is placed all the way through a definite process of subset production. The subsequent set is placed through the procedure to test its performance.

   If this performance endures the anticipated conditions, then it will be designated as the final subset. Otherwise, the deriving subset will once more be placed through the procedure of subset generation for more fine-tuning.

9.7.2 Feature Extraction

In this technique, features or sovereign variables from the given set of data are renovated into novel self-governing variables called as new feature space. Freshly assembled feature space clarifies most data and only momentous data are preferred.

Let a set consist of n number of features say, $X_1.......X_n$. After feature extraction, there are m attributes where $(n > m)$ and this feature extraction is completed with a few mapping function, F.

X_n which consists of a set of independent features or dimensions is condensed to Y_n set of independent features which is referred to in Figure 9.4. In this extraction process, a method named principal component analysis is implemented. This will acquire only non-redundant and significant features from X_n and transform into fresh feature space Y_n. With this technique, the ability of interpretation is misplaced because, Y_n features acquired after feature extraction are not equal to X_n, which means it is not a direct subset of X_n.

9.7.3 Naïve Bayes

This particular classifier classifies by using Bayes theorem to categorize the data. This accepts the probability of definite feature X which is entirely solitary of the other feature Y as shown in Equation 9.1.

$$P(Defect\,|\,Machine\ B) = \frac{P\big(Machine\ B\,|\,Defect\big) * P\big(Defect\big)}{P\big(Machine\ B\big)} \qquad (9.1)$$

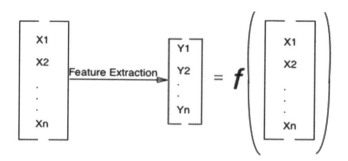

FIGURE 9.4

X_n Set of independent features or dimensions are reduced to Y_n.

Bayes theorem provides a way to anticipate the probability of the assumption given that there is a former knowledge regarding the problem given by Equation 9.2.

$$\text{Posterior} = \frac{\text{Likelihood} * \text{Prior}}{\text{Evidence}} \qquad (9.2)$$

9.7.4 AdaBoost

This is a booming approach scheduled by Freund and Schapire as shown in Figure 9.5. AdaBoost (adaptive boosting) is the most widely implemented boosting algorithm. Boosting is an amalgamation method which is used for constituting extremely precise estimation or durable classifier from comparatively scrawny and imprecise classifiers. This algorithm is a process of iteration where a model is skilled in data and estimates frail learners.

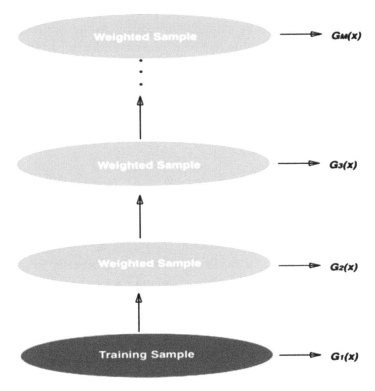

FIGURE 9.5
Schematic of AdaBoost.

Let the samples for the training be 20 in a binary categorization problem and there should be evenly separated training samples, *D1*. Let *w* be the initial weight of each and every sample which is 1/20. Subsequent to the training samples which are trained in a model *G1*, 5 of them are wrongly categorized. Henceforth, error rate $e = 0.25$, the weight of model *G1* is shown in Equation 9.3

$$G_{1 = \alpha = \frac{1}{2}} \left(\frac{1-e}{e} \right)$$

(9.3)

Correctly classified samples are weighted low by multiplying with *e*QTS and the misclassified samples are weighted further by multiplying with *e*TS and finally all weights are normalized to 1. Currently, the next model is trained *G2* and the similar procedure persists till best possible samples are suitably classified and last model is the addition of every weighted models. The schematic of AdaBoost is given in Figure 9.5.

The foremost set of self-determining predictor variables, which are to be modeled, is training sample. Subsequent to the achievement of the modeling error rate, the feeble learners are identified. Those novice feeble learners are weighted and the samples are once again modeled. These procedures persist up to *M* number of times and at last all the outputs from various samples are averaged to produce the boosted output.

9.8 RESULT

Here, python (Anaconda Application) programs have been used for the prediction of the output data. Similarly, it is not necessary to uninstall Pandas and Numpy, since these are all default packages that are found in the software platform.

The initial step for a programming is to insert the dataset into the program. The dataset has been collected from the sensors that consist of various parameters like voltage, temperature, vibration, pressure, etc. The result has been predicted with the help of python. It is determined that ANN works well with the industrial predictive analysis and the results are evaluated as follows.

9.9 EVALUATION

The true positives and true negatives are the crucial diagonal line in the confusion matrix. Performance metrics can be derived from the confusion matrix. Accuracy can be determined by employing Equation 9.4:

$$\text{Accuracy} = TP + TN / TP + TN + FP + FN \times 100\% \qquad (9.4)$$

The True Positive (TP) rate is the percentage of positive cases that were appropriately recognized (Maharajan and Paramasivan 2019) by Equation 9.5.

$$\text{Recall} = TP / TP + FN \times 100\% \qquad (9.5)$$

The Precision is the percentage of the expected positive cases that were precise (Maharajan and Paramasivan 2019) by Equation 9.6.

$$\text{Precision} = FP / FP + TN \times 100\% \qquad (9.6)$$

Detection time: In order to recognize an attack packet during detection, detection time is employed and a short detection time is considered as better detection time.

9.10 ANALYSIS

The comparison of all the classifiers employing the method of cross-validation with score feature and without score feature is given in the Table 9.1 and Figure 9.6.

TABLE 9.1

Comparison of Classifiers Employing the Method of Cross-Validation

Evaluation Criteria	Classifiers with the Score Features			Classifiers without the Score Feature		
	Naïve Bayes	SVM	ANN	Naïve Bayes	SVM	ANN
Accuracy (%)	94.53	95.52	97.01	74.62	79.10	82.08
Sensitivity (%)	87.87	96.96	96.96	60.60	81.81	81.81
Specificity (%)	97.05	94.11	97.05	74.66	82.35	82.35

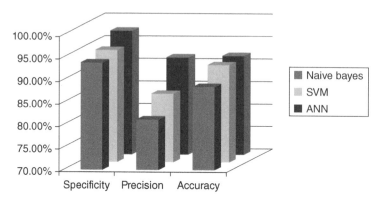

FIGURE 9.6
Comparison of classification accuracy.

Following cross-validation, it was found that the best performance for each classifier was 94.53% for Naïve Bayes, 95.52% for SVM, and 97.01% for proposed classifier as shown in Figure 9.6 It is found that among classifiers, Naïve Bayes and SVM, the proposed method performs better with the classification accuracy of 97% when tested with cross-validation. Moreover, the model also improves classification quality in terms of both sensitivity and specificity employing a better feature vector. As mentioned earlier, the false alarm rate could also be easily detected by this algorithm. This could be done effectively with ANN and the predicted graph.

9.11 CONCLUSION

This chapter estimated the accuracy, precision, and specificity. Finally, a detailed analysis was made between these approaches to determine the best method to be used to overcome some of the current industrial predictive maintenance challenges. In SVM model, the training/test samples are represented as dot/points in the space and they are mapped in such a way that the clear gap among the categories which separate the samples. The need to model many complicated functions is with the same idea that gave rise to the concept of ANN. The technique behind learning is that it interactively determines the coefficients for the input and the output that leads to the prediction. For the function approximation as stated in the previous sentence, it is not necessary for the neural network to fit into a straight line. The extension of the function approximation arises with the forecasting that predicts the time series data. We have a target variable and if that value predicts the same point in future time, then at each step of the training phase we should present the historical data to the neural network. ANN and IoT work well with the sample classification that maps the input data with the various categories and classes.

10

IoT Integration in Blockchain for Smart Waste Management

10.1 A BRIEF INTRODUCTION OF WASTE MANAGEMENT

In urban areas, enormous waste around the globe is confronting a typical issue, dealing with the city waste adequately without making city unclean. The present waste management systems include countless workers being designated to go to a specific number of dumpsters. This is done every day. This gives a wasteful and unclean system wherein a few dumpsters will flood a few dumpsters probably won't be even half full. This is brought about by a variety in populace thickness in the city or some other arbitrary factor which makes it difficult to figure out which part needs prompt consideration.

Waste is characterized as any material where something important isn't being utilized or isn't usable to its proprietor (Mahajan et al 2017).

Depending upon the physical condition of the waste, they are ordered as (Maheswari et al 2019):

1. Strong Waste
2. Wet Waste

With the multiplication of populace, the situation of neatness as for waste management has progressed toward becoming essential. Waste management incorporates arranging, accumulation, transport, treatment, reuse, and transfer of waste under an observation and guideline (Mahajan et al 2017).

Waste management is the process of planning and making necessary arrangement to dispose the waste efficiently with less manpower and at affordable cost. There are many methods that are implemented to dispose, recycle, and reduce wastes but still there are challenges associated with them such as practical implementation as per the society needs. It is wise to choose the methods appropriately as per the requirements of the people.

This undertaking manages the issue of waste management in shrewd urban areas, where the garbage gathering system isn't upgraded. This task empowers the associations to address their issues of intelligent garbage management system. This system enables the client to realize the fill level of every garbage container in a region or city, to give a practical and efficient course to the truck drivers.

10.1.1 Challenges in Waste Management

It is not the role of one individual to manage and make a change immediately in waste management; it is duty of all the people over the globe to do the necessary changes.

Few of the challenges that are needed to be addressed are:

- Awareness and knowledge
- Waste separation at source
- Huge volume of waste generation
- Technology upgrade
- Construction of landfills
- Accountability in waste management
- Tracking E-Waste

10.1.2 Awareness and Knowledge

One of the principle explanations for the waste administration begins with an absence of mindfulness. The people producing the waste need mindfulness on why and how to isolate waste, when all is said and done; there is an absence of mindfulness about effects of inappropriate waste administration on wellbeing and nature. The challenges in waste management are shown in Figure 10.1.

10.1.3 Waste Separation at Source

The primary resources of waste are family units and enterprises were isolation of waste at source is required. Directly, the greater part of the waste

FIGURE 10.1
Challenges in waste management.

arriving at the network or region container is not appropriately isolated as biodegradable and non-biodegradable waste.

The waste created builds step by step in unfathomable manners. Waste age is corresponding to pay per capita of the nation. In low-center salary nations, increment in human population has increment in waste generation.

The sources of waste generation is shown in Figure 10.2.

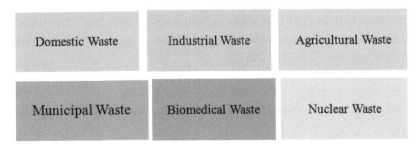

FIGURE 10.2
Classification of waste.

10.1.4 Technology Upgrade

Waste generators and waste handlers don't have the great idea of how and where the wastes are dealt with once they leave their container. There is no legitimate following framework for waste administration. In spite of the fact that innovation like Radio-frequency identification (RFID) is utilized for waste administration, its use is constrained. In current waste administration framework, information is entered physically which would prompt information blunder making irregularities and wrong information section and control of information for the monetary profits. Furthermore, official letters are passed as physical paper that could get lost during the travel.

10.1.5 Construction of Landfills

Present-day landfills are not built deductively as they pollute groundwater and contaminate the air through methane gas emission. Terrible smell, fire blast, and rummaging of creatures is among different issues experienced at landfill destinations. The quantity of accessible landfill destinations isn't keeping pace with the nation's interest. Over 70% of gathered urban waste is dumped straight into the landfills.

10.1.6 Accountability in Waste Management

There is presently a feeling that the present waste management framework– by purchasers and companies–lacks a feeling of accountability leading to frustration with reusing endeavors. No digital transaction framework as of now exists to consider companies or individuals accountable for the waste they've created and lost reusing. By placing makers, purchasers, and waste management operators into a system together, blockchain could create a perspective on the waste supply chain that is accessible and noticeable (Kumar et al 2016). Blockchain adds value to both the customer and the company by demonstrating individual impact to each individual from the system (Huh et al 2017).

10.1.7 Tracking E-Waste (E-Waste Management EWM)

EWM is the process of disposing of e-waste in an environmental friendly manner (Gupta and Bedi 2019). The initial step involves collection of electronic waste items from the consumers, followed by arranging it into

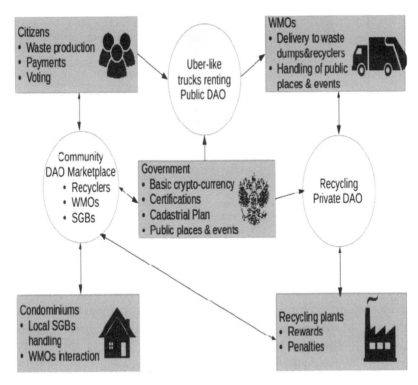

FIGURE 10.3

DAO Enables formation of different kinds of organization on top of blockchain.

reusable and non-reusable items. The reusable items are kept for resale while the non-reusable items are disassembled (Kushwaha et al 2014). Figure 10.3 shows that Decentralized Autonomous Organization (DAO) enables the formation of different kinds of organization on top of blockchain (Lamichhane et al 2017).

10.2 WASTE MANAGEMENT USE CASE

Figure 10.4 shows the cycle of waste management where the wastes are collected initially from the people and then they will be segregated as per the classification of waste, then the classified wastes are transported to the available location for the processing (Gupta and Bedi 2019).

Here, people must join each other for making waste management DAO in the locations. The two major technologies are Internet of Things (IoT)

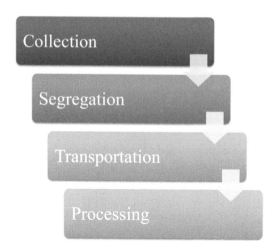

FIGURE 10.4
Waste management cycle.

and blockchain technology. Several tools such as Arduino, Kinoma, M2MLabs Mainspring, Node-RED, BeagleBoard, Flutter, LightBlue Bean Punch Through, Microduino, OpenPicus, Pinocci, and RasWIK were being evolved with the concept of IoT technologies (Annamalai and Udendhran 2019).

10.3 PRIOR ART

People of many countries spend their maximum cost in disposing the waste since the garbage has been collected in the larger trucks and it is carried to the recycle plants or landfill sites. But many countries spend maximum cost in the waste production and spend less in their disposal (Annamalai and Udendhran 2019). The waste percentage ratios are shown in Table 10.1.

TABLE 10.1

Waste Percentage Ratios

S. No.	Percentage Ratio	Description
1	36	Recycle
2	47	Burning Calories
3	10.2	Landfilled

Many solutions have been found by IoT devices for these challenges. Message Queuing Telemetry Transport (MQTT) or Constrained Application Protocol (CoAP) are used mostly in an environment that achieves maximum efficiency of energy (Annamalai and Udendhran 2019).

10.4 DISPOSE WASTE EMPLOYING TAG

User needs to dispose waste using Thrift and Green (TAG); therefore, the user requires two main things:

1. A Telegram App
2. An Ethereum account

From the Ethereum Wallet user can download and register with an Ethereum account. The entire facility of the DAO could be found in the TAG that runs with the common currency activated by a central bank (Lamichhane et al 2017; Annamalai et al 2019). The status of waste generation is shown in Figure 10.5.

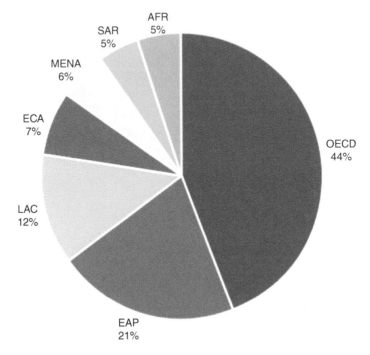

FIGURE 10.5
Waste generation status.

10.4.1 IoT Protocols in MQTT

MQTT has been used as it possesses increased bandwidth and power economic protocol to monitor the waste management (Lamichhane et al 2017). Transmission Control Protocol/Internet Protocol TCP/IP protocol has been used for this communication establishment (Annamalai and Udendhran 2019). The components of MQTT are shown in Figure 10.6.

The main features are as follows:

1. Asynchronicity
2. Open standard
3. Multiplexing multiple subscribers through a single channel

Necessary Quality of Service (QoS) is also provided based on the message delivery service provided (Lamichhane et al 2017). It used a TCP connection in all places (Annamalai and Udendhran 2019).

MQTT has three categories such as

- Subscriber
- Broker
- Publisher

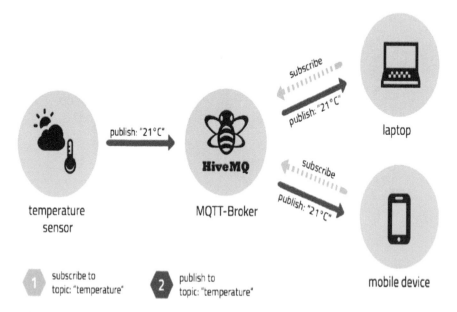

FIGURE 10.6
Components of MQTT.

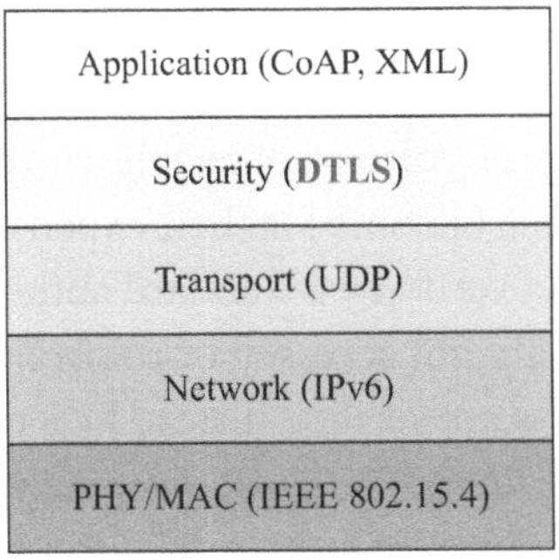

| Application (CoAP, XML) |
| Security (DTLS) |
| Transport (UDP) |
| Network (IPv6) |
| PHY/MAC (IEEE 802.15.4) |

FIGURE 10.7
CoAP Protocol.

10.4.1.1 MQTT Broker

It acts as a bridge between the message sender and the receiver. It makes enough provisions to end the process by getting the messages and ensuring the particular message topic from the rightful receivers (Annamalai and Udendhran 2019; Lamichhane et al 2017).

10.4.1.2 Subscriber

The message will be received by every client who will subscribe to a topic and the broker will deliver the matching topic of all the messages to the client (Annamalai and Udendhran 2019). The layers in CoAP Protocol are shown in Figure 10.7.

10.4.1.3 Publisher

Here the message will be sent from publisher to MQTT by the process called as publishing. It comprises of sensors, gateways, and other embedded devices for the message transmission (Lamichhane et al 2017).

10.5 BLOCKCHAIN-DRIVEN WASTE MANAGEMENT

It is a block of chains, where the blocks are digital information and chain is public database. The aim of blockchain is to permit digital information must be recorded and distributed, whereas it cannot be edited. Blockchain technology was started in 1991 by Stuart Haber and W. Scott Stornetta, who implemented a method in which document timestamps cannot be tracked. It has taken 20 years to reach its objective.

Globally, there is a large population of people who possess Bitcoin, and people of any country can use bitcoins for their expenses. With printed money, currency is regulated and verify by a standard authority, such as the government; however, bitcoins are not accessed or controlled by any one governing body and the transactions are verified instead by a network of computers.

Blockchain is the distributed database system that interacts with several nodes, which will maintain all the records and transactions in a chronologically with more security. With this system, interaction of intermediate systems is not necessary, which will transfer the data in a secure layer thus lowering the costs. Bitcoin has been the most thriving implementation of blockchain (Annamalai and Udendhran 2019).

10.6 BLOCKCHAIN AND IoT

Blockchain and IoT are the two emerging technologies that have reduced the work of manpower in many places. In solid waste management, they play a dominant role in the management of solid waste. IoT is the interconnection of the devices or the sensors that enable the users to know the about any abnormal activities that are happening in their environment. The connectivity in Blockchain and Internet of Things is shown in Figure 10.8.

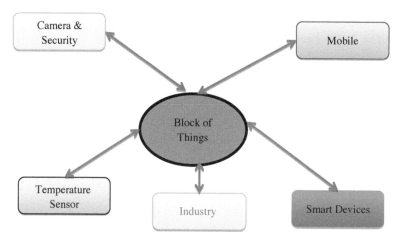

FIGURE 10.8
Blockchain and Internet of Things.

The challenging factor in IoT is the security and privacy as the Internet is connected throughout the time. Here, the blockchain can be associated with it to match the security issues of IoT. The detailed architecture is shown in Figure 10.8.

The major features of blockchain include:

- Decentralization
- Anonymity
- Security

Each spending day, the world is suffocating under the expanding volume of waste, efficiently affecting human wellbeing, atmosphere, and condition. Systematic and effective waste management has showed up as an extreme test influencing many creating nations. Expanded pace of urbanization and populace and fast advancements are answerable for the age of the monstrous measure of waste. The developing waste age rates, the issues of finding new disposal sites, depletion of landfill space, and waste disposal and management techniques are hampering sufficient waste management (Joseph 2014).

10.6.1 Swachhcoin

It is a blockchain-based approach for micromanagement of wastes from family units and businesses and changing over them into helpful items in an effective and eco-accommodating manner. Power, paper, steel, timber, valuable metals, and glass plastics are a portion of the high financial value yields from the handled wastes. The swachh biological system is a DAO, administered autonomously on the basis of predefined directions as the smart contracts. Swachhcoin utilizes numerous cutting-edge technologies to execute an iterative procedure cycle, which over some undefined time frame will make the framework totally autonomous, proficient, and profitable. This iterative procedure cycle centers around the data exchanged between various actors in the biological system, analyzing these data and giving recommendations in real time, based on prescient techniques (Gopalakrishnan and Ramguru 2019).

SwATA (Swachh Big Data):

1. SwATEL (Swachh Adaptive Intelligence)
2. SwIoT (Swachh Internet of Things)

TABLE 10.2

Waste Management Techniques

S. No.	Techniques	Working
1	SwATA (Swachh Big Data)	Customized application collects stores and analyses these data like routes optimization and report generation.
2	SwATEL (Swachh Adaptive Intelligence)	Adaptive Intelligence (AI) to decide decisions on previous learning
3	SwIoT (Swachh Internet of Things)	A landfill can be connected and controlled by IoT.
4	SwBIN (Swachh Bins)	If waste is deposited, SwBIN will identify the user with UID and measure quantity and quality of waste check the reward points.
5	Swachh Tokens	They are utility tokens where a user receives a reward for better waste management.

  3. SwBIN (Swachh Bins)
  4. Blockchain and Smartcontracts
  5. Swachh Tokens

The waste management techniques (Gopalakrishnan and Ramguru 2019) is given in Table 10.2.

10.6.2 Recereum

It is a blockchain platform for transforming waste and recyclables into real value. This blockchain makes direct communication between the clients and the waste gathering organization. Recereum biological system is operating on the largest open blockchain Ethereum. Blockchain records the rewards starting with one account then onto the next account. The main applications as stated in the Recereum whitepaper are smart contracts, payments, and supply chain management (Gopalakrishnan and Ramguru 2019).

10.6.3 Plastic Bank

It is a blockchain-based application with the mission to stop the progression of plastic into the ocean, by adapting individuals. The plastics gathered through this initiative are reused and sold as Social Plastic. These Plastic Bank confirmed plastic that gave a premium to the authority as rewards. These rewards are conveyed, authenticated, and put away utilizing

Blockchain innovation to give the safest and most believed means to convey a globally scalable social impact (Gopalakrishnan and Ramguru 2019).

For proficient outcomes, it is vital to present a cutting-edge waste management system to see a full cycle of waste management, from how they were gathered to when and where they were discarded. Blockchain waste management platform could be utilized by the waste management specialists to accomplish supportable sanitation. Additionally, interfacing IoT sensors (gauge sensors and RFID) with the decentralized system can create the information and offer continuous following office of the garbage trucks all through their voyage (Debiao and Zeadally 2014).

10.7 CONCLUSION

IoT-based services were implemented in the waste management but still there are practical implementation issues and the cost is high as it is done by a third party. Moreover, the government could not afford enough funds to raise an advanced management equipment and system. IoT combined with blockchain helps in managing the waste efficiently and recycling it properly. This method may seem a little bit tough, but it can be more efficient than any other mechanism.

References

Adelson, D. "Intelity forecast of hotel technology in 2017." (2016).

Ahmed, M., M. Björkman, and M. Lindén. "A generic system-level framework for self-serve health monitoring system through Internet of Things (IoT)." In pHealth, (2015): 305–307.

Alam, J., and M. K. Pandey. "Design and analysis of a two stage traffic light system using fuzzy logic." Journal of Information Technology and Software Engineering 5, no. 162 (2015): 2.

Al-Fuqaha, A., M. Guizani, M. Mohammadi, M. Aledhari, and M. Ayyash. "Internet of Things: A survey on enabling technologies, protocols, and applications." IEEE Communications Surveys & Tutorials 17, no. 4 (2015): 2347–2376.

Ali, S., and K. A. Smith. "On learning algorithm selection for classification." Applied Soft Computing 6, no. 2 (2006): 119–138.

Altin, M., Z. Schwartz, and M. Uysal. ""Where you do it" matters: The impact of hotels' revenue-management implementation strategies on performance." International Journal of Hospitality Management 67 (2017): 46–52.

Andersson, P., and L. G. Mattsson. "Service innovations enabled by the 'Internet of Things'." IMP Journal 9, no. 1 (2015): 85–106.

Anguelovski, I.. "From toxic sites to parks as (green) LULUs? New challenges of inequity, privilege, gentrification, and exclusion for urban environmental justice." Journal of Planning Literature 31, no. 1 (2016): 23–36.

Annamalai, S., and R. Udendhran. "An efficient framework based on cloud computing integrated with Internet of Things technology for intelligent waste management." In Novel Practices and Trends in Grid and Cloud Computing, pp. 132–145. IGI Global, Pennsylvania, 2019.

Annamalai, S., R. Udendhran, and S. Vimal. "Cloud-based predictive maintenance and machine monitoring for intelligent manufacturing for automobile industry." In Novel Practices and Trends in Grid and Cloud Computing, pp. 74–89. IGI Global, Pennsylvania, 2019.

Araújo, J., M. Mazo, A. Anta, P. Tabuada, and K. H. Johansson. "System architectures, protocols and algorithms for aperiodic wireless control systems." IEEE Transactions on Industrial Informatics 10, no. 1 (2013): 175–184.

Atzori, L., A. Iera, and G. Morabito. "The Internet of Things: A survey." Computer Networks 54, no. 15 (2010): 2787–2805.

Balaji, M. S., and S. K. Roy. "Value co-creation with Internet of Things technology in the retail industry." Journal of Marketing Management 33, no. 1–2 (2017): 7–31.

Barratt, M. J., J. A. Ferris, and S. Lenton. "Hidden populations, online purposive sampling, and external validity: Taking off the blindfold." Field Methods 27, no. 1 (2015): 3–21.

Bello, J.J., 2018. "IoT in Retail: 7 Real Examples." Ubidots Blog.

Bok, B. G. J. "Innovating the retail industry: An IoT approach." Bachelor's thesis, University of Twente, 2016.

Brody, P., and V. Pureswaran. "The next digital gold rush: How the Internet of Things will create liquid, transparent markets." Strategy & Leadership 43, no.1 (2015): 36–41.

Brown, R. R., M. A. Farrelly, and D. A. Loorbach. "Actors working the institutions in sustainability transitions: The case of Melbourne's stormwater management." Global Environmental Change 23, no. 4 (2013): 701–718.

Brown, R. R., N. Keath, and T. HF Wong. "Urban water management in cities: Historical, current and future regimes." Water Science and Technology 59, no. 5 (2009): 847–855.

Byun, J., and D. Kim. "Oliot EPCIS: New EPC information service and challenges towards the Internet of Things." In 2015 IEEE International Conference on RFID (RFID), pp. 70–77. IEEE, San Diego, CA, USA, 2015.

Capel, H. El m. Barcelona: Un examen crítico. Ediciones del Serbal, Barcelona, 2005.

Carlson, C., O. Barreteau, Paul Kirshen, and Kim Foltz. "Storm water management as a public good provision problem: Survey to understand perspectives of low-impact development for urban storm water management practices under climate change." Journal of Water Resources Planning and Management 141, no. 6 (2014): 04014080.

Chan, HCY. "Internet of Things business models." Journal of Service Science and Management 8, no. 04 (2015): 552.

Chen, JKC, Y. W. Yu, and J. Batnasan. "Services innovation impact to customer satisfaction and customer value enhancement in airport." In Proceedings of PICMET'14 Conference: Portland International Center for Management of Engineering and Technology; Infrastructure and Service Integration, pp. 3344–3357. IEEE, New Jersey, 2014.

Chesa, M. J. "Stormwaer management in Barcelona. Evolving approaches." In Baltic Flows Conference. Barcelona, vol. 17. 2016.

Contreras, J. I., F. Alonso, G. Cánovas, and R. Baeza. "Irrigation management of greenhouse zucchini with different soil matric potential level. Agronomic and environmental effects." Agricultural Water Management 183 (2017): 26–34.

Cousins, J. "Volume control: Stormwater and the politics of urban metabolism." Geoforum 85 (2017): 368–380.

Cousins, J. "Of floods and droughts: The uneven politics of stormwater in Los Angeles." Political Geography 60 (2017): 34–46.

Dasgupta, A., R. Nagaraj, and K. Nagamani. "An Internet of Things platform with google eddystone beacons." Journal of Software Engineering and Applications 9, no. 06 (2016): 291.

de Haan, F. J., B. C. Rogers, N. Frantzeskaki, and R. R. Brown. "Transitions through a lens of urban water." (2015): 1–10.

Dijkman, R. M., B. Sprenkels, T. Peeters, and A. Janssen. "Business models for the Internet of Things." International Journal of Information Management 35, no. 6 (2015): 672–678.

Dlamini, N. N. "The potential use of the Internet of Things (IoT) in South African retail businesses." PhD diss., University of Cape Town, 2017.

Domènech, L., H. March, M. Vallès, and D. Saurí. "Learning processes during regime shifts: Empirical evidence from the diffusion of greywater recycling in Spain." Environmental Innovation and Societal Transitions 15 (2015): 26–41.

Dumitrache, I., and S. I. Caramihai. "The intelligent manufacturing paradigm in knowledge society." In Knowledge Management. IntechOpen, 2010.

Elish, K. O. and M. O., Elish. "Predicting defect-prone software modules using support vector machines." Journal of Systems and Software 81, no. 5 (2008): 649–660.

Ettlinger, M., and K. Gordon. "The importance and promise of American manufacturing." Center for American Progress (2011).

Feldman, B., E. M. Martin, and T. Skotnes. "Big data in healthcare hype and hope." Dr. Bonnie 360 (2012): 122–125.

Ferretti, M., and F. Schiavone. "Internet of Things and business processes redesign in seaports: The case of Hamburg." Business Process Management Journal 22, no. 2 (2016): 271–284.

Firdausi, A. "Overview the Internet of Things (IoT) system security, applications, architecture and business models." Universitas of Electrical Engineering, Indonesia, 2016.

Fong, L. H. N., R. Law, C. M. F. Tang, and M. Hong Tai Yap. "Experimental research in hospitality and tourism: A critical review." International Journal of Contemporary Hospitality Management 28, no. 2 (2016): 246–266.

Furlong, C., K. Gan, and S. De Silva. "Governance of integrated urban water management in Melbourne, Australia." Utilities Policy 43 (2016): 48–58.

Gandino, F. M., B. Montrucchio, and Maurizio Rebaudengo. "Key management for static wireless sensor networks with node adding." IEEE Transactions on Industrial Informatics 10, no. 2 (2013): 1133–1143.

Gerpott, T. J., and S. May. "Integration of Internet of Things components into a firm's offering portfolio – a business development framework." Info 18, no. 2 (2016): 53–63.

Gubbi, J., R. Buyya, S. Marusic, and M. Palaniswami. "Internet of Things (IoT): A vision, architectural elements, and future directions." Future Generation Computer Systems 29, no. 7 (2013): 1645–1660.

Gupta, N., and P. Bedi. "E-waste management using blockchain based smart contracts." In International Conference on Advances in Computing, Communications and Informatics (ICACCI), pp. 915–921. IEEE, New Jersey, 2018.

He, D., and S. Zeadally. "An analysis of RFID authentication schemes for Internet of Things in healthcare environment using elliptic curve cryptography." IEEE Internet of Things Journal 2, no. 1 (2014): 72–83.

Huh, S., S. Cho, and S. Kim. "Managing IoT devices using blockchain platform." In 2017 19th international conference on advanced communication technology (ICACT), pp. 464–467. IEEE, New Jersey, 2017.

Islam, S. M. R., D. Kwak, M. D. H. Kabir, M. Hossain, and K. Kwak. "The Internet of Things for health care: A comprehensive survey." IEEE Access 3 (2015): 678–708.

Jayalakshmi, M., and V Gomathi. "Pervasive health monitoring through video-based activity information integrated with sensor-cloud oriented context-aware decision support system." Multimedia Tools and Applications (2018): 1–14.

Jayalakshmi, M. and Gomathi, V. "Sensor-cloud based precision agriculture approach for intelligent water management." International Journal of Plant Production (2019): 1–10.

Jeeradist, T., N. Thawesaengskulthai, and T. Sangsuwan. "Using TRIZ to enhance passengers' perceptions of an airline's image through service quality and safety." Journal of Air Transport Management 53 (2016): 131–139.

Joseph, K. "Municipal solid waste management in India." In Municipal Solid Waste Management in Asia and the Pacific Islands, pp. 113–138. Springer, Singapore, 2014.

Karthikeyan, S., R. Patan, and B. Balamurugan. "Enhancement of security in the Internet of Things (IoT) by using X. 509 authentication mechanism." In Recent Trends in Communication, Computing, and Electronics, pp. 217–225. Springer, Singapore, 2019.

Krauss, C., X. A. Do, and N. Huck. "Deep neural networks, gradient-boosted trees, random forests: Statistical arbitrage on the S&P 500." European Journal of Operational Research 259, no. 2 (2017): 689–702.

Krawczak, M. Multilayer Neural Networks: A Generalized Net Perspective, Vol. 478. Springer, Singapore, 2013.

Kshetri, N. "The economics of the Internet of Things in the global south." Third World Quarterly 38, no. 2 (2017): 311–339.

Kumar, P., A. Sarangi, D. K. Singh, S. S. Parihar, and R. N. Sahoo. "Simulation of salt dynamics in the root zone and yield of wheat crop under irrigated saline regimes using SWAP model." Agricultural Water Management 148 (2015): 72–83.

Kumar, T. V., and B. Dahiya. "Smart economy in smart cities." In Smart Economy in Smart Cities, pp. 3–76. Springer, Singapore, 2017.

Kumar, V., M. Amorim, A. Bhattacharya, J. A. Garza-Reyes, G. C. Parry, S. A. Brax, R. S. Maull, and I. CL Ng. "Operationalising IoT for reverse supply: The development of use-visibility measures." Supply Chain Management: An International Journal (2016).

Kushwaha, A. K., N. Gupta, and M. C. Chattopadhyaya. "Removal of cationic methylene blue and malachite green dyes from aqueous solution by waste materials of Daucus carota." Journal of Saudi Chemical Society 18, no. 3 (2014): 200–207.

Lamichhane, M., O. Sadov, and A. Zaslavsky. "A smart waste management system using IoT and blockchain technology." Master's thesis, ITMO University, 2017.

Lee, I., and K. Lee. "The Internet of Things (IoT): Applications, investments, and challenges for enterprises." Business Horizons 58, no. 4 (2015): 431–440.

Lee, W.-H., and C. C. Cheng. "Less is more: A new insight for measuring service quality of green hotels." International Journal of Hospitality Management 68 (2018): 32–40.

Lee, Y.-K., and J.-Woo Park. "Impact of a sustainable brand on improving business performance of airport enterprises: The case of Incheon International Airport." Journal of Air Transport Management 53 (2016): 46–53.

Li, C., J. Lei, Y. Zhao, X. Xu, and S. Li. "Effect of saline water irrigation on soil development and plant growth in the Taklimakan Desert Highway shelterbelt." Soil and Tillage Research 146 (2015): 99–107.

Li, X. "Vegetation establishment in coastal salt-affected wasteland using drip-irrigation with saline water." Land Degradation & Development 30 no. 12 (2019): 1423–1436.

Li, X, Y. Kang, S. Wan, X. Chen, and L. Chu. "Reclamation of very heavy coastal saline soil using drip-irrigation with saline water on salt-sensitive plants." Soil and Tillage Research 146 (2015): 159–173.

Liphoto, T. S. "Internet of Things-based traffic management system for Maseru, Lesotho." PhD diss., Central University of Technology, Free State, Bloemfontein, 2017.

Litman, T. "Smart congestion relief: Comprehensive analysis of traffic congestion costs and congestion reduction benefits." https://www.vtpi.org/cong_relief.pdf (2016).

Lopes, T. A. P., and N. F. Ebecken. "In-time fatigue monitoring using neural networks." Marine Structures 10, no. 5 (1997): 363–387.

Lykou, G., A. Anagnostopoulou, and D. Gritzalis. "Smart airport cybersecurity: Threat mitigation and cyber resilience controls." Sensors 19, no. 1 (2019): 19.

Mahajan, S. A., A. Kokane, A. Shewale, M. Shinde, and S. Ingale. "Smart waste management system using IoT." International Journal of Advanced Engineering Research and Science 4, no. 4 (2017).

Maharajan, K., and Paramasivan, B. "Membrane computing inspired protocol to enhance security in cloud network." The Journal of Supercomputing 75, no. 4 (2019): 2181–2192.

Maheswari, R., H. Azath, P. Sharmila, and S. S. R. Gnanamalar. "Smart village: Solar based smart agriculture with IoT enabled for climatic change and fertilization of soil." In 2019 IEEE 5th International Conference on Mechatronics System and Robots (ICMSR), pp. 102–105. IEEE, New Jersey, May 2019.

Moss, T. "Conserving water and preserving infrastructures between dictatorship and democracy in Berlin." Water Alternatives 9, no. 2 (2016).

Munir, A., P. Kansakar, and S. U. Khan. "IFC IoT: Integrated fog cloud IoT: A novel architectural paradigm for the future Internet of Things." IEEE Consumer Electronics Magazine 6, no. 3 (2017): 74–82.

Murray, A., A. Papa, B. Cuozzo, and G. Russo. "Evaluating the innovation of the Internet of Things: Empirical evidence from the intellectual capital assessment." Business Process Management Journal 22, no. 2 (2016): 341–356.

Neeba, E. A., J. Aswini, and R. Priyadarshini. "Leveraging the Internet of Things (IoT) paradigm towards smarter applications." In Novel Practices and Trends in Grid and Cloud Computing, pp. 306–324. IGI Global, Pennsylvania, 2019.

Newe, G. "Delivering the Internet of Things." Network Security 2015, no. 3 (2015): 18–20.

Ng, W. W., D. S. Yeung, M. Firth, E. C. Tsang, and X. Z. Wang. "Feature selection using localized generalization error for supervised classification problems using RBFNN." Pattern Recognition 41, no. 12 (2008): 3706–3719.

Nolin, J., and N. Olson. "The Internet of Things and convenience." Internet Research 26, no. 2 (2016): 360–376.

Omina, J. A. "An intelligent traffic light control system based on fuzzy logic algorithm." International Academic Journal of Information Systems and Technology 1, no. 5 (2015): 1–17.

Padrón, S., D. Guimarans, J. J. Ramos, and S. Fitouri-Trabelsi. "A bi-objective approach for scheduling ground-handling vehicles in airports." Computers & Operations Research 71 (2016): 34–53.

Palattella, M. R., M. Dohler, A. Grieco, G. Rizzo, J. Torsner, T. Engel, and L. Ladid. "Internet of Things in the 5G era: Enablers, architecture, and business models." IEEE Journal on Selected Areas in Communications 34, no. 3 (2016): 510–527.

Pang, Z., Q. Chen, W. Han, and L. Zheng. "Value-centric design of the Internet-of-Things solution for food supply chain: Value creation, sensor portfolio and information fusion." Information Systems Frontiers 17, no. 2 (2015): 289–319.

Peng, S. L., S. Pal, and L. Huang. Principles of Internet of Things (IoT) Ecosystem: Insight Paradigm. Springer, Singapore, 2020.

Pigni, F., G. Piccoli, and R. Watson. "Digital data streams: Creating value from the real-time flow of big data." California Management Review 58, no. 3 (2016): 5–25.

Pramanik, M. I., R. Y. K. Lau, H. Demirkan, and Md. A. K. Azad. "Smart health: Big data enabled health paradigm within smart cities." Expert Systems with Applications 87 (2017): 370–383.

Preethi G., and R. Ramaguru. "Blockchain based waste management." International Journal of Engineering and Advanced Technology (IJEAT) ISSN: 2249 – 8958, 8, no. 5, (June 2019).

Raj, P., and P. Evangeline. The digital twin paradigm for smarter systems and environments: The industry use cases, volume 117, 2020.

Raj, P., and A.C. Raman. Intelligent Cities: Enabling Tools and Technology. Auerbach Publications. 2015.

Singh, A., S. Pal, and G. K. Jha. "Transitioning India's public expenditure in agriculture towards higher growth and equity." Indian Journal of Agricultural Economics 70, no. 902-2016-68390 (2015): 246–258.

Sklyar, T., and E. Sokolova. "Driving forces for information and communication technology innovations in smart health in St. Petersburg." In IOP Conference Series: Materials Science and Engineering (Vol. 497, No. 1, p. 012094). IOP Publishing, 2019.

Sotoca, J. M., and F. Pla. "Supervised feature selection by clustering using conditional mutual information-based distances." Pattern Recognition, 43, no. 6 (2010): 2068–2081.

Straker, K., and C. Wrigley. "Translating emotional insights into digital channel designs: Opportunities to enhance the airport experience." Journal of Hospitality and Tourism Technology 7, no. 2 (2016): 135–157.

Suresh, A., R. Udendhran, and G. Yamini. "Internet of Things and additive manufacturing: Toward intelligent production systems in industry 4.0." In Internet of Things for Industry 4.0, pp. 73–89. Springer, Cham, 2020.

Tossell, D. "Developing your digital guest strategy." Hotel Executive (2015).

Turner, B. "When big data meets big brother: Why courts should apply United States v. Jones to protect people's data." NCJL & Tech 16 (2014): 377.

Venkatesh, P., M. L. Nithyashree, V. Sangeetha, and S. Pal. "Trends in agriculture, non-farm sector and rural employment in India: An insight from state level analysis." Indian Journal of Agricultural Sciences 85, no. 5 (2015): 671–677.

Vermesan, O., P. Friess, P. Guillemin, R. Giaffreda, H. Grindvoll, M. Eisenhauer, M. Serrano. "Internet of Things beyond the hype: Research, innovation and deployment." IERC Cluster SRIA (2015).

Vo-Dinh, T., P. Kasili, and M. Wabuyele. "Nanoprobes and nanobiosensors for monitoring and imaging individual living cells." Nanomedicine: Nanotechnology, Biology and Medicine 2, no. 1 (2006): 22–30.

Yahyaoui, I., F. Tadeo, and M. V. Segatto. "Energy and water management for drip-irrigation of tomatoes in a semi-arid district." Agricultural Water Management 183 (2017): 4–15.

Yang, Y., J. Lei, W- Zhang, and C. Lu. "Target classification and pattern recognition using micro-doppler radar signatures." In Seventh ACIS International Conference on Software Engineering, Artificial Intelligence, Networking, and Parallel/Distributed Computing (SNPD'06), pp. 213–217. IEEE, New Jersey, 2006.

Yousefpour, A., C. Fung, T. Nguyen, K. Kadiyala, F. Jalali, A. Niakanlahiji, J. Kong, and J. P. Jue. "All one needs to know about fog computing and related edge computing paradigms: A complete survey." Journal of Systems Architecture. (2019).

Zhang, M., Z. Ma, Yan Z., and Y. Wang. "An identity authentication scheme based on cloud computing environment." Multimedia Tools and Applications 77, no. 4 (2018): 4283–4294.

Zhang, X., J. Li, Y. Liu, Z. Zhang, Z. Wang, D. Luo, X. Zhou. "Design of a fatigue detection system for high-speed trains based on driver vigilance using a wireless wearable EEG." Sensors 17, no. 3 (2017): 486.

Zhong, C.-L., Z. Zhu, and R.-G. Huang. "Study on the IoT architecture and gateway technology." In 2015 14th International Symposium on Distributed Computing and Applications for Business Engineering and Science (DCABES), pp. 196–199. IEEE, New Jersey, 2015.

Index